RICHARD WALKER &
RELATIONSHIP EQUITY

If you have the good fortune to fall into Richard Walker's orbit you first are caught in a whirlwind of charisma. Only later, slowly, do you realize the depth of his perception and selflessness. You will reconsider your closely held patterns of behavior. He will improve you as he has me and many others — prince and pauper alike — who flock to him for advice.

STEVEN J. KERN
MD FACS

The snazzy shoes, big smile, gregarious laugh, and welcoming arms are the epitome of Richard Walker; a true master of connecting others through selfless purpose and drive. I have watched Richard for over two decades build relationships where people feel truly valued, inspired to connect with other and give back to make the communities they come from a better place. What you see is what you get with Richard — a genuine, charismatic leader who puts the value of a relationship before everything else. Our world is better because of Richard, and *Relationship Equity* is a masterful composition of doing just that.

KIM SKANSON
President, Cargill

I have known Richard for over a decade, and he has been a great friend and mentor to me. He is also one of the most successful and generous leaders I have ever met. In *Relationship Equity*, he reveals the secret behind his remarkable achievements: building strong and lasting relationships with everyone he meets. This book is not only a fascinating story of his journey from bricklayer to CEO, but also a practical guide on how to create meaningful connections in life and business. If you want to learn from the best, read this book. You won't regret it.

FRANÇOIS CHARETTE
Enterprise CTO, Optum

Richard Walker has been one of the most influential people on the trajectory of my career, as he called out in *Relationship Equity*, he taught me the value of investing in my professional and personal network. Through our relationship, Richard helped guide me from being a middle manager to a c-level executive at a $20 billion public company. In the process, I learned that paying it forward, without expectation will give you more gratification in life than any professional achievement.

MARC KERMISCH
Chief digital and information officer, CNH Industrial

Richard Walker is the real deal. *Relationship Equity* isn't just a book, it's how Richard approaches life. As a recipient of Richard's relationship equity, I know firsthand the impact this has had on me and so many others. In *Relationship Equity*, Richard reveals the principles that propelled his success personally and professionally. From his humble beginnings to his successful career, his story can be your playbook.

MARK W. MURPHY
Executive vice president and chief information and digital officer, 3M

As an executive, fellow immigrant, and life coach, Richard's story truly resonated with me. *Relationship Equity* speaks volumes to those of us that value team collaboration and see its long-term ability to achieve great results. I thoroughly enjoyed the personal stories which at times had me laughing out loud. However, I have walked away with a deepening connection to the importance of continuing to build and foster relationships!

KELLEY GURLEY, PH.D
Global head of data digital technology portfolio and demand management, Takeda

Richard is interested in every person. That is clear in your first interaction. He genuinely wants to know more about you, and then, how he can help you.

He is a giver. He gives of his time, his talents, and he shares his valuable relationships. He is always looking to connect individuals and develop people to help everyone become the best they can be.

I have been the benefactor of Richard giving me one of the most precious items of his, no it is not Guinness or Jameson (although I have been the benefactor of those too), or his golf tips (of which I have received many), it is of his time. He has taken time to get to know me and to connect me to others whom he thought might be helpful with whatever I was addressing. In return, I have gladly given my time for introductions to help others and develop individuals at all levels in his network. I have found it incredibly rewarding to help him in the work he does for our youth and younger professionals.

He is a pebble in the ocean of relationships. He has no idea of the distance and size of the ripples he has created. They have crossed the ocean many times over. Thank you, Richard.

JOHN NAYLOR
CEO, Medica

The consummate relationship-builder, Richard Walker has built a career (and a life) through his innate ability to connect with others. His colorful personality, flashy wardrobe, and self-deprecating sense of humor may initially get your attention, but one soon discovers that beneath the surface lies a man of real substance. As authentic, humble, unselfish, and caring as they come, Richard epitomizes what it means to be a servant leader, and I'm thrilled Richard has chosen to share his insights and perspectives on relationship-building with us all.

JEFF TOLLEFSON
Resident and CEO, Minnesota Technology Association

I'm guessing anyone who has met Richard would agree he is a bit different. Many people probably wonder if this guy is for real. *Why does he want to help me? What is in it for him?* Helping others is what gets him up in the morning. It is in his soul.

I've always believed you reap the seeds you sow. What Richard brought to me and our company is the absolute belief and dedication that we need to invest in our relationships with our York team members and our IT community without regard to what the upside is for us. We must do it because helping others is the right thing to do.

Richard likes to say we do well by doing good. Truth is, he thrives on helping others succeed in life and business. More importantly, he is not just a good business partner, but is a great friend.

It would be an understatement to say we have had our ups and downs in business. But there is nobody I would rather take that ride with than Richard.

I have no doubt *Relationship Equity* will have a profound impact on those who read it.

BILL CARR
Chairman of the board, York Solutions

Your Cornerstone
Investment
to Great Gains
in Business and Life

RELATIONSHIP
EQUITY

RICHARD
WALKER

Forbes | Books

Published by Forbes Books, Charleston, South Carolina.
An imprint of Advantage Media Group.

Forbes Books is a registered trademark, and the Forbes Books colophon is a trademark of Forbes Media, LLC.

Printed in the United States of America.

10 9 8 7 6 5 4 3 2 1

ISBN: 978-1-95588-439-6 (Hardcover)
ISBN: 979-8-88750-014-0 (eBook)

Library of Congress Control Number: 2023907637

Cover design by Matthew Morse.
Layout design by Matthew Morse.

This custom publication is intended to provide accurate information and the opinions of the author in regard to the subject matter covered. It is sold with the understanding that the publisher, Forbes Books, is not engaged in rendering legal, financial, or professional services of any kind. If legal advice or other expert assistance is required, the reader is advised to seek the services of a competent professional.

Since 1917, Forbes has remained steadfast in its mission to serve as the defining voice of entrepreneurial capitalism. Forbes Books, launched in 2016 through a partnership with Advantage Media, furthers that aim by helping business and thought leaders bring their stories, passion, and knowledge to the forefront in custom books. Opinions expressed by Forbes Books authors are their own. To be considered for publication, please visit **books.Forbes.com.**

To my little brother, Johnny:

I hope my book makes its way up to heaven, as the way you lived your life epitomizes every aspect of it. You lit up every room you walked into. And lit up the opposition (in a very different way) on every rugby field you stepped foot on. Your quick wit always had those around you doubled over in laughter. You are, and always will be, sorely missed.

CONTENTS

INTRODUCTION: "WE'RE ALL JUST PEOPLE"

"Do you think other people are better than you?" my father asks me.

I am a lad of ten, and he is sitting next to me on the sidelines of the football field where my team has just lost a match. I'm alternating between moping and sputtering out excuses and insults against my teammates, our opponents, or both—but he will hear none of it.

"Do you think they're better than you, son?" he repeats calmly.

"Of course they are, Dad!" I answer, rolling my eyes and kicking at the dirt. "We lost, didn't we? I mean, you saw the score for yourself, right?" And I begin another round of excuses.

He cuts me short. "No, they're not better. And if you start thinking others are better than you, that means you're thinking you're better than others, and you're not. We're all just people, Richard. Sure, there's always going to be some who have better skills, but that doesn't make them better people. Never forget that."

And I never have. Half a century later, I realize those were some of the most profound words that I have ever heard. It was a lesson about respect for others and for myself. My father was teaching me to accept everybody as individuals of value, one way or another. To recognize that value, I would have to get to know them. I would need to build relationships.

This is a book about building relationships, in life and in business, and how we all can benefit from treating others with the sort of respect that my parents imparted to my brother, sister, and me. When you regard others with goodwill, they tend to regard you the same way and reciprocate.

Growing up in Settle, a town in Northern England where the sheep outnumbered the people, I learned the fundamental values of respect, teamwork, accountability, and character—but most of all hard work. Today, those are the same values that we emphasize at York Solutions, an IT consulting firm based in Minneapolis, Minnesota, that I started with a partner, Bill Carr, in 1998. It is what I do, and I care deeply for my profession, but it does not define me. What defines me is my ability to connect with others and help to improve their lives, professionally and personally.

One good turn deserves another is an expression dating back hundreds of years and, no doubt, is a sentiment as old as humanity. Aesop had more than one fable in which ants and birds and other critters helped one another out of danger and into prosperity. That expression captures the essence of Relationship Equity, which we will examine in the chapters ahead.

Not to oversimplify the moral of the story, though. There are numerous nuances to the concept that I have learned throughout my life and career. It's not so simple, and it doesn't come easily or naturally. It often goes against what might be considered conventional wisdom. It requires patience, dedication, and intentionality. Even then, there's no guarantee of a positive outcome. It is, nonetheless, worth every moment of the effort.

Relationship Equity is the good faith that you can build up in your relationships by investing in them faithfully and steadily, without expectation of reaping a return. Quite often, though, when you keep adding deposits to a relationship bank account, you end up with a profitable return. I have seen it happen, over and over.

It's not quid pro quo, though. Relationship Equity isn't about mutual back-scratching. It's about mutual growth and not just business growth—relational growth. The emphasis is on forging stronger bonds with others, truly understanding their wants and needs. It's a mindset that can work wonders in families, marriages, and communities.

> Relationship Equity is the good faith that you can build up in your relationships by investing in them faithfully and steadily, without expectation of reaping a return.

It comes down to this: When you do right by others, they will likely want to do right by you. A tangible benefit may not come right away—it may not come at all. But that's not the point. You win because word gets around about your character, and that's what builds the momentum for mutual success. People take an interest in you because you have taken an interest in others. They want to be around a team player.

Sounds simple, right? It's not. To gain a high level of equity in a relationship takes time, dedication, and a fair portion of good luck—but when those efforts succeed, the dividends can be remarkable. When you show genuine interest in others, that interest compounds.

I owe so much to my upbringing. My father, Richard Walker II (which—obviously—makes me the III), worked in the same creamery factory for nearly forty years and is the wisest man I know. My mother, Luigina, immigrated from a farm in southern Italy in her early twenties to seek a better life as a cleaner in an expensive boarding school. She couldn't speak a word of English when she met my father at a dance there. In fact, she hadn't even known other languages existed until leaving home. I can't imagine how they communicated, but it seems love is a universal language. She has been my lifelong source of inspiration because of the courageous way she took control of her life at such a young age.

My parents never missed one of our football, rugby, or cricket games, though they were polar opposites in their approach. My father never said a word as he watched our matches. He studied every play with his steel trap of a mind, and win or lose, his demeanor didn't change. It was a constant no matter how well I played. Conversely, my mother, true to her exuberant heritage, would shout from start to finish from the sidelines and occasionally from out in the field.

I recall a middle school football game when she vaulted a fence to get between me and another kid as we were squaring off. And we still tease her about the time she swatted a rugby player with an umbrella after he got into a tussle with my brother, Johnny, at one of his professional matches. ("That's just not true!" she objects. "I didn't have my umbrella. It was my handbag.") Like my father, she was a champion for fair treatment. She just pursued different methods.

And this memory, too, comes back to me often: I am eight years old and have been chosen to be the goalie in a school football match. The weather is dismal. I am shivering and begin to cry. And suddenly my mother is next to me, wrapping her coat around me, and I am in her arms, and we are going home. All she cared about, and has ever cared about, was the welfare of her family. And that, no doubt, is the most important value that both my parents instilled in me.

As I look back, I am amazed by where life has taken me. Born in 1966, I am the eldest of three kids in our family. My brother, Johnny, the rugby pro, tragically passed away in 2013 at the age of forty-four when a blood clot in his leg led to a pulmonary embolism. My sister, Gillian, still lives in Settle and has owned her own hairdressing business since she was eighteen years old. She is continuing her entrepreneurial pursuits by opening a new clothing shop and recently earned a degree in psychology. When we were growing up, the word *college* didn't seem to be in anyone's vocabulary, though all three of us eventually pursued degrees.

At the time, the expectations for my future were clear and were established by the environment in which I was born. I was expected to leave high school at the age of sixteen and find work, most likely at one of the five local factories, one of which was the creamery. It was what people in my world did. It is what my friends did, and it is what I did. However, once I became of age, my father informed me that I would not be working at the creamery, no way. So I found a job as a bricklayer with a local construction company.

I worked hard as a bricklayer and took the job seriously—though it was as far away from the world of IT as a person could get, by geography as well as technology. Hard work was not a problem for me. Whatever I do, I try to do it well, and I resolved to be the best bricklayer in town, specializing in stone fireplaces.

Young people often limit themselves to what they have come to believe is their lot in life. They conform to what is expected of them or what they imagine is expected. The gravitational pull of environment and upbringing can be as strong as an ocean's tide. The cycle can continue for generations.

But I was yearning for something more—something beyond the world I knew, though I had no idea what or how I would find a future away from grueling work in the drizzle and chill of rural England. I knew that I didn't want to become like my older coworkers who had begun to experience the physical effects of a lifelong livelihood in manual labor. But I didn't know where to go from there or how to break the cycle.

For years after I started a new life in America, I tried to hide my background instead of wearing it proudly. I felt like an impostor who could never fit in. I had grown up observing all around me that a life of toil was my model for manhood. I felt like an outsider masquerading in the white-collar world. Then one day I had an epiphany as I recalled my father's words: *Do you think others are better than you, Richard?* No longer would I be held captive to that limiting notion. Through the years, I have met many who likewise feel unworthy. It's called imposter syndrome, and it stifles people's potential.

> We rise, or we fall, on the quality and strength of our relationships.

As I advanced into adulthood, I witnessed the power of Relationship Equity firsthand. At so many turns, I met people who graciously gave me attention, advice, and encouragement. They believed in me. I have done my best to return their investment in our relationship—and with interest.

What fascinates me the most is discovering ways to positively influence the lives of others, as others have done for me. This is not so much a business book as it is a philosophy book. What I offer here is a game plan not only for good business but also for good living. To be best at both, we must develop reliable and authentic connections with others. That's what engenders growth. That's what promotes prosperity. Only by reaching outward and upward can we move onward. We rise, or we fall, on the quality and strength of our relationships.

Come with me now on a journey of discovery. In the pages ahead, I will tell the tale of how those relationships took me from being a bricklayer in a small town in Northern England to the CEO of a successful American IT company. Throughout the stories I share, you will see the power of a principle through which you can build a better business—and, more importantly, you can open opportunities to help others build better lives.

INVESTING IN HUMANITY

Wayne Gretzky, the great ice hockey legend, was once asked why he scored more goals than everybody else each season. He answered, "I don't go to where the puck is. I go to where it's going to be."

That's the sort of winning way that we all would do well to emulate. He didn't just react swiftly. He anticipated. The first takes skill and good reflexes. The second requires wisdom, foresight, and acceptance of the risk.

In 1997, I was working in my first job in the IT industry at a small company in Saint Louis, Missouri. About a year into that job, my boss asked me if I would be willing to move to Chicago to start a new division that would focus on IT contracting services. My wife,

Lisa, and I were just starting a family. We had a one-year-old and one on the way, but we agreed that yes was the right answer.

In Chicago, as I was setting up the office in a temporary space, a chap named Bill Carr stopped by to chat. He had just started his own business as a headhunter for IT companies in need of employees and was interested in what I was doing in town. I took a quick liking to this guy and told him briefly about my company's plan to launch IT contracting services. Then I noticed he was wearing a golf tie. The business talk ceased, and the golf stories commenced. Golf has a way of taking over a conversation. I had a distinct feeling, early on, that something good was going to come from this relationship.

When we did get around to talking business again, Bill began asking a flurry of questions. He had no idea that I had such limited experience. He presumed that since I had been sent to open an office, I must know what I was doing. Frankly, I didn't even know that I didn't know what I was doing. Still, Bill kept picking my brain, trying to pull out what little was up there. And, to my surprise, I was actually able to answer most of his questions.

A few hours later, we were still talking. He told me he wanted to open a contracting and consulting business using the same business model that I was starting in Chicago. In other words, he planned to be a direct competitor to me. He would be going after the same resources and people that I needed to bring aboard—so why the hell would I help him do that?

I could have said no. I could have said, "Sorry, mate, I have other fish to fry." I suppose that would have been a sensible reaction. I looked at him closely. "Absolutely," I said. "Tell me what I can do for you."

Bill asked for my help setting up contracts, and we consulted regularly as I helped him launch a business that would be in direct competition. Why would I do that? I can't say that there was any logic to it. It just seemed right to me, so I trusted that gut feeling. I was there for him, and our relationship deepened. Golf played no small part in the equation.

A year or so later, Lisa and I returned to Saint Louis. One day, out of the blue, Bill called.

"Richard, I want to start a new business, and I want you to come in as a partner, okay? I want you to help me build it. Would you be willing to do that?"

I listened to the details. He wanted us to expand on the consulting/contracting business model. He told me that I would earn equity as the new company grew, but he didn't expect me to put up any money up front. And that was good because I didn't have a proverbial pot to piss in. Lisa and I were just getting started and facing the expenses of a young family.

That was 1998. Together, Bill and I proceeded to build York Solutions, play plenty of golf, and become dear friends for a lifetime. When Bill took a step back in 2015, I assumed the role of chief executive officer. Our friendship remains strong. We meet on the golf course at least every other week, and business talk seldom comes up these days. Why should it? He's retired and confident in my leadership. The equity of a long and trusting relationship has granted us the freedom to laugh in the sunshine.

None of that would have happened if I had not agreed, beyond all logic, to help him back in Chicago. I can't say my brain had the best pickings in town, but as we worked together, Bill could see that our complementary skill sets would make a strong team.

"Skills come second," Bill would say. "First I want to know who someone is as a person."

Just because someone is highly educated and well trained doesn't make them a better person. Nothing wrong with education, of course, and strong skills are essential in IT, as in any industry, but what he looked for first was what was in the heart and soul. It was a mindset in keeping with the way I had been raised as a boy back in North Yorkshire.

I had met a chap who would come to influence me through the years as few others have done. His emphasis consistently was on helping others to truly succeed, and that required more than a set of skills. When we met, I was well on my way, sure, but Bill must have recognized my relative inexperience. Nonetheless, he also recognized something else in me that soon would make him want me as a business partner. He didn't go to where the puck was. He went to where it was going to be. As a result, together we have been successful in building a strong and profitable business.

The bottom line here is the power of relationships. In the business world, as in virtually all human affairs, relationships are of paramount importance. I have seen through the years, over and over, how successful relationships contribute mightily to business growth. I have not noticed so much that business growth, on its own, breeds successful relationships.

> Fostering strong, sacrificial, respectful relationships mutually benefits everyone; this truth is the foundation of Relationship Equity.

The most important equity you can build is the human touch. When you show others that you genuinely care and want to help, they more often than not want to reciprocate. That's a fundamental principle—not only in business but also in our families and in our world. Fostering strong, sacrificial, respectful relationships mutually benefits everyone; this truth is the foundation of Relationship Equity.

Think of Relationship Equity as an investment. It isn't one that, necessarily, will build your bank account, though it quite often does. Rather, the equity you are building is in people. You are investing in relationships because you believe it's the right thing to do. Whether or not it results in dollars and cents, it always makes good sense to get to know people on an equal footing, not expecting a payback but exploring how you can help one another. And when you are open to that, marvelous things tend to happen.

"We're all just people," my father told me when I was young. We possess differing skills, but those skills don't define us as a better or a lesser person. To become our best, we must reach out to others and put those abilities together for our mutual strength and benefit. You can't do that unless you get to know people first. Building equity in relationships requires a genuine desire to extend the hand of friendship. It requires getting to know people for who they are and what they can become.

At York Solutions, we practice that philosophy. In this book, we will examine programs that are creating unprecedented opportunities in the IT world. I will share stories about our endeavors not to demonstrate how grand I am but to suggest how better off we all would be by investing in others from a place of genuine concern.

> To become our best, we must reach out to others and put those abilities together for our mutual strength and benefit.

"People before profits" doesn't mean settling for one or the other but rather embracing both. Your network is often equivalent to your net worth. The people we surround ourselves with play a large role in our success.

This book is not a primer on IT intricacies, though much of it involves people in my industry. Rather, this book will teach you about the importance of Relationship Equity, a principle with power to revitalize every field as well as our personal lives. Collectively, we could be tapping into a wealth of potential that we have yet to realize. Relationship Equity can change lives, and that is why I have written this book.

THE RELATIONSHIP EQUITY MINDSET

Two men, both named Ted, were competing for a promotion for a top executive job at a major corporation. Independent of each other, both men asked for my coaching when applying for the role. After the decision was made, I had the opportunity to chat with them separately.

"You must be disappointed," I told the first Ted. "Why do you think you didn't get the job?"

"It's because I just refuse to kiss the backsides of everyone, the way that other guy does," he said. "If my track record isn't good enough, then it's their loss."

I asked the second Ted why he thought he got the job. "The main thing," he answered, "was that I spent the last year forging relationships with top executives, providing as much value to them as I could. I got to know the people who make things happen and spent a lot of time with them finding out what they needed and how I could help them."

So there you have it. The first Ted figured his technical talents would take him all the way. And sure, he was good at his job, but there is more than one kind of track record. The second Ted was smart, too, and not just at executing projects. He understood the importance of creating authentic relationships, which in turn created trust. He knew the right things to say to the right people, at the right time, for the right reasons. He was promoted because, all else being equal, he had gained the respect and trust of the ultimate decision makers.

Teamwork calls for a cooperative and helpful spirit that focuses on the interests of the group, not the self-interests of the individual. It's all about *us*, not *me*. To work cooperatively means, by definition, that you are not just in it for yourself. You only win if the team wins. Any personal gain results from reciprocation borne of appreciation.

Your attitude can be your making or breaking. Some people are naturals at building Relationship Equity, and that springs from the belief system instilled in them during childhood. If the adults model a mindset that it is good to reach out to others, the kids will catch on. The default, unfortunately, often is much more self-focused. The prevailing sentiment is *What's in it for me?*—and the kids catch on to that, too.

A common perception is that the most successful among us are those who look out for number one. It pays to be selfish, people tend to think. They believe that selfless souls earn less money. Do they? That perception has been examined. A 2020 study titled "Generosity Pays," published in the *Journal of Personality and Social Psychology*, set out to determine whether people who put a priority on self-oriented behavior did better in life. The researchers' polling had determined that 68 percent of the public believed that was true. The study analyzed thousands of survey answers from both Americans and Europeans and identified which of them were the most selfish on the basis of their responses. Then the study looked at those people's income and family size. The selfish ones, as a whole, earned less and had fewer children.[1]

The mindset of Relationship Equity clearly advances one's success not only professionally but also personally. It is the discipline of thinking about others before self. When you do that, good things often come to you in return. Think of it as winning all around—and what you win often will be modest. What you gain from helping others might not be some grand promotion or business deal. It often is as simple as feeling good about what you have done to make someone else's world even a little better. For many people, that is motivation enough.

Nobody's a Mind Reader

As a favor to a friend—who happened to be the chief operating officer at a global manufacturing conglomerate—I once helped a young woman land a great job. A few months later, she told me she was feeling frustrated. She had pitched the idea of bringing in tech contractors, but she hadn't been able to find any.

"Well, why didn't you call *me*?" I asked her.

"Why would I call you?"

"Uh, because that's what we *do* here," I said. She didn't know. I had never made that clear to her. She may well have wanted to show appreciation for my help, but I hadn't let her know how she could do that.

---

1   K. Eriksson, I. Vartanova, P. Strimling, and B. Simpson, "Generosity Pays: Selfish People Have Fewer Children and Earn Less Money," *Journal of Personality and Social Psychology* 118, no. 3 (2020): 532–44.

As a result, I instituted a change in how we do things at York Solutions, where we talk a lot about Relationship Equity. As we develop relationships, I pointed out, we should be letting people know, in one way or another, how they could specifically help us if they chose to do so. And most people do. Not always but usually. They want to reciprocate—but we no longer expect them to be mind readers.

Moving in New Circles

Without our connections to others, what would become of us? Would we be a race of hermits living in cliff caves, venturing out only to forage at dusk? I suppose some would find that appealing, but the vast majority of us are social beings who need others. We are creatures of connection. The Relationship Equity mindset seeks to make the most of those connections.

Most of what is written about networking is about transactional dealings, and, true, that is the extent of the connection you will have with many people whose paths you cross. You only have so much of yourself to go around. You cannot have deep interpersonal relationships and abiding friendships with everyone you know. Instead, you will have an inner circle of such people, with everyone else outside that core. Some will be closer in, some will be farther out on the fringes, some will be floating in distant orbit.

RELATIONSHIP EQUITY CIRCLE

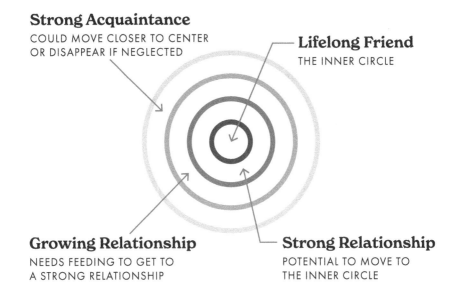

Strong Acquaintance
COULD MOVE CLOSER TO CENTER
OR DISAPPEAR IF NEGLECTED

Lifelong Friend
THE INNER CIRCLE

Growing Relationship
NEEDS FEEDING TO GET TO
A STRONG RELATIONSHIP

Strong Relationship
POTENTIAL TO MOVE TO
THE INNER CIRCLE

In fact, a good way to understand Relationship Equity is as a series of inner and outer circles on a chart. Every person you ever have known would occupy a position on that chart. Within the innermost circle will be the proven few who are with you for the long haul. You have infinite equity with them on a deep emotional level. These are your lifelong friends and devoted family members—the people you could call in a crisis and know they would be at your side in a heartbeat. Just beyond that layer, clustered around the perimeter of the inner circle, are other friends and associates you have come to know well and with whom you have built mutually rewarding relationships. You get together now and then, but the equity that you have built in those relationships can easily erode over time unless you continually feed it.

The closer the relationship is to the inner circle, the more equity you have built with that person. The farther out the relationship is from the core, the more it is merely transactional, based on the exchange of services or money. Maybe it's the guy who mows your lawn. Maybe it's the person whose hand you once shook at a conference as you exchanged business cards with a polite smile. Nothing wrong with that, of course. My point is to acknowledge that most relationships are limited and don't advance very far.

Some do, though. Relationships are not static. They thrive when nurtured, and they shrivel when neglected. Like a master gardener, you must know what needs the most attention, how much, and when. Who prefers the bright sun, and who does better in the shade? And you need to get in there and yank out the weeds before they choke the growth.

In other words, relationships require effort. They are forever in motion. You can always count on the forever faithful ones who have made it to your inner circle, but the others will at times come closer and at times edge away. Occasionally a passing acquaintance will swoop in like a comet to brighten your world before drifting off again. That is the nature of Relationship Equity: you don't always know what to expect, but it is good to build it anyway.

When Relationship Equity becomes your mindset, when you practice those skills daily until they become reflex, you can be sure that you will find yourself moving in new circles with opportunities possible at every step.

Creating those connections can be a learned skill. Even if it doesn't come naturally, you can master the art with practice. The more you share about yourself, the greater the opportunity to find those connections. Look for common ground: *Oh, you went to that school? So did I. What did you study? Oh, you like to play golf? Me too. I live for golf!* Once you find a connection, the conversation comes easier. Such simple commonalities usually are the spark that ignites a relationship. Within minutes you can feel like old pals.

You might think that this approach is obvious and natural, but for many people it is not. They hold their cards close to the vest. They are slow to open up. We are all wired differently, so sometimes finding that common ground can be difficult—but, again, it is worth the effort. When Relationship Equity becomes your mindset, when you practice those skills daily until they become reflex, you can be sure that you will find yourself moving in new circles with opportunities possible at every step.

The Right Questions

"Here are a few questions that I want you to ask the candidate who's coming in this afternoon," my boss told me. It was my first job in the IT field, working as a recruiter. This was supposed to be a temporary position while I took night school classes to become a physical education teacher. I didn't intend to get into the IT industry—it sort of happened by default.

The CEO of that company, based in Saint Louis, was a fella named Brad Layton. When he interviewed me for the position, I had no clue what the IT world was about. Still, he saw something in me. He wanted to hire somebody who understood people and who could ask the right questions.

One of those questions, though, I was reluctant to ask. "When the candidate comes in," Brad told me, "be sure to find out how much money he is making. He's looking for a new job." Brad could tell from the look on my face that I wasn't keen on doing that. That was how I was brought up: it's just not polite to talk about money that way.

I mumbled something about how the question might seem too personal. "Well, you'd *better* ask him that," Brad said, "because if you don't, you're not going to be able to help him."

That's when it clicked. My job was to help people—and if the candidate was already making $50,000 a year, what good would it do him if we suggested a position paying $30,000? I would be wasting his time and mine. To be helpful is my prime directive, and I understood that I needed to adjust my belief system.

You need to ask plenty of questions to learn about people, but that is not to say that all questions are appropriate. Always be sure to say the right things, at the right time, to the right people, in the right way. To this day, when I meet somebody new, I don't jump right in with the typical question of "So what do you do for a living?" I am sensitive to how that comes across to some folks, since for a long time, I felt that disclosing my bricklaying days would forever pigeonhole me. I feared people wouldn't see beyond that.

That is why I believe that it is always better to find some other point of connection first and to consider the true purpose of your questions. Are you aiming to be helpful? If you don't know why you are asking, don't ask. If you are just curious, be patient. Always ask questions with the intention of listening and understanding; responding is secondary. Consider your body language in all interactions, especially the first time you are meeting with someone. Are you engaged in what they are saying, or are you distracted by something in your world? Is it clear to the other person that you are interested in hearing what they have to say? Be intentional about steering the conversation in the other person's direction.

These are all aspects of human interaction that are too commonly overlooked. They garner trust and respect. You need to go slow enough so that people can see your values and intentions. That will make them want to share theirs.

When It "Just So Happens ..."

In the corporate world, many relationships develop for a specific purpose. It's hardly surprising that you will get to know the people you see every day on the job, and if you are together on a team, you have a purpose in common. Businesspeople intentionally build relationships with others in their industry. They know what they want, and they make it happen.

In our social lives, though, many relationships seem to happen randomly. They can grow from the smallest of seeds that you did not even know you were planting. I once started chatting with a chap simply because I noticed that he was holding a pint of Guinness. We hit it off so well that, a decade later, we went together to Augusta to witness Tiger Woods win the 2019 Masters. Today, Chris is most definitely in my inner circle, as I am in his. And to think—it all started over a pint of black liquid and a smile.

Later in this book, I will spin a few tales about my beloved North Captiva Island in Florida, where my family has a home. Golf carts are the way we get around there, and I often stop to offer a lift to folks I encounter strolling along the sand pathways. That has led to rewarding relationships—such as with two gentlemen I met who were in the construction business, a rare find on the island. Had I just rolled on past, would we ever have connected?

Each of us could tell stories about chance encounters that changed the course of our lives. You meet someone who introduces you to someone who has an idea—or some version of that sequence. And decades later, your world looks far different on account of those random strokes. Is the path we take in life merely a matter of luck? Some of it is. But so much depends on what you do with that luck once it comes your way. The opportunity is just the starting point.

What matters most is what comes next. Do you roll on past? Or do you just say yes?

I think back on how I met my wife. I had come to the States for a summer camp job as a golf instructor, and afterward I spent some time exploring the country before returning to England. I still have the ticket stubs from my thirty-one flights on a Delta Air Pass. While airborne, I liked to chat with other passengers. They would ask me about where I was heading or where I'd been. "The Grand Canyon!" I would say, or "Niagara," or "Vegas."

On one of those later flights, after visiting such delightful destinations, I proclaimed: "I'm heading to Tulsa, Oklahoma!" Silence. Their puzzled expressions said it all: *What would possess you to go there?*

Well, my new buddy Roy from the summer camp was attending Oral Roberts University in Tulsa, and it so happened that we decided to go to the same bar where a young lady named Lisa Hennessy and her friends also decided to go that evening, at the same hour. And it so happened that this particularly engaging young lady overheard my accent and liked it, even if she got it wrong. Randomness. A lot of things in life *just so happen.* But she and I did something with the opportunity that came our way. We *made* things happen—and still are, thirty-three years later.

The Give and Take

The Relationship Equity mindset isn't some fancy formula that requires calculations and ruminations. It's about as simple as it gets. It comes down to thinking first about helping others get what they hope to achieve and then letting them help you with what you hope to achieve.

2: THE RELATIONSHIP EQUITY MINDSET

Human nature being what it is, though, people tend to think first and more highly of themselves—and when that is the case, it all stops there. To get what we want, we each need the assistance and cooperation of others, but if we were all takers instead of givers, who could accomplish anything? Nobody wins if nobody is willing to help. Nothing wrong with a healthy ego, as long as your self-awareness button is switched on. A successful relationship always requires a little give and take.

> A successful relationship always requires a little give and take.

A business relationship can develop into a personal one, and vice versa, and that is all well and good. There should be no barriers between the two, despite the conventional wisdom that suggests otherwise. Family and career are two of the most important elements of all of our lives, so a good way to help people is likely to be found in one or the other. When you set strict boundaries between those worlds, you rule out possibilities for how you can help others and for how they can help you. I have had business relationships develop into lifelong friendships, and I have fostered friendships that led to mutually rewarding business deals. In every case, the primary focus was the giving and not the receiving, as sweet as the latter can be.

Only a good friend, it's often said, will tell it to you straight—and isn't straight talk highly valued in the world of business? No matter how frank the discussion, true friends will always know you have their best interests at heart. Friends can tell each other not only what they want to hear but also what they need to know. That only works, though, if you have plenty of equity in the relationship. If you don't, you can say the wrong thing to the wrong person at the wrong time, and your straight talk could be taken the wrong way.

The more equity you have in a relationship, the more you can dish it out, and the more you will be willing to get dished. I joke that I try to treat everyone with the same level of disrespect. Good-natured ribbing is a hallmark of a good friendship, and quite often the teasing delivers a much-needed message.

This is the much-needed message I hope to deliver in this book: You must be intentional about creating Relationship Equity. It will take you to new heights in your career, in your family, and in your community. If you hope to attain what you are capable of achieving, it's high time to adopt the mindset that will be the foundation for your success.

FOUNDATIONS OF
A PHILOSOPHY

Let us now go back in time so that you can better see where I am coming from. I will introduce you to some folks who helped me along the way, even when they seemed to have no reason for doing so. In kindness and in the spirit of helpfulness, they tried to do what was best for me. They were laying the foundation for my philosophy of Relationship Equity. These are the kind of people who would be inclined to help not just me but you, too, and who would encourage you to do likewise for others.

One such soul was my boss back in Settle who taught me, a wild-haired teenager, how to use a trowel and a level to render a heap of rocks into a thing of beauty. I need only close my eyes, and it is 1984 again. I am heading out for another day of plying my trade, my work pants stained with yesterday's mortar, my hands rough from two years of hefting stones. My boss, Bernard Smith, approaches me as I arrive at the job site.

"Hold on there a moment, Richard," he says. "I want to ask you about something you should be thinking about."

"Yes, Mr. Smith?" We step aside, and he fixes his eyes on me.

"So why the hell are you a bricklayer?" His words do not exactly sound encouraging to me.

"Wha—why am I?" I feel flustered. *What kind of question is that?* I get defensive.

"Because that's what I was supposed to do," I blurt out, scowling. "And I thought I was good at it."

"I'm not doubting that you are," he says with a trace of a smile. "I just want you to know, Richard, that there are so many things you could be doing besides what you're doing here."

I have no idea what he means. My thoughts race. *Am I not doing enough for him? Do I need to master a new set of skills to earn my pay? Has someone been complaining about me? Is he about to fire me?*

From the perspective of years, I understand how much this man simply wanted me to know that he saw something in me and that he felt I should aspire to other things. At the time, it just felt that he didn't want me on the job anymore. I knew I had what it took. What I lacked was the confidence that others knew it, too.

As it turned out, what he wanted instead was my help. He wanted me to work with him at a youth club that he operated a couple of times a week and on the weekends. It sounded intriguing. I said yes to the opportunity, and it wasn't long before I took over as the primary youth leader, working with the kids at the club. I was only nineteen, which was two years younger than the regulations allowed, but the club made an exception for me.

I often wonder what I would be doing today if I had said no to his offer, believing that I shouldn't venture beyond the confines of a life that seemed to have been cut and pasted into place for me. Sure, I was good at bricklaying, and I had every reason to be proud of my skills, but would I ever have discovered whether I was good at anything else? At what cost to self and society does a person fail to explore other gifts within?

A few years later, in 1988, the youth service approached me and asked whether I might be interested in going to the United States as a camp counselor and a golf instructor through an organization called Camp America.

That would mean I would have to leave my bricklaying career for four months with no guarantee of getting my job back. Again, the yes came quickly. I didn't consider turning down this opportunity. America, seriously? What an adventure! I had never traveled far from my doorstep, aside from the few times I visited my family in Italy. And golf? You might say that golf is a game that is built into my DNA. Little did I know, at the time, how that decision to travel to America would change my course, and my life, and the lives of others, forever.

Those four monumental months in a brave new world nearly four thousand miles away passed swiftly. I returned to my hometown of Settle and went straight back to the familiar patterns of working at my old job and with the youth club. My attitude was much different now. I was a changed man.

Though I still had no idea what I would do in life, it was clear to me that there was much more for me out there. Everything was temporary. After putting the final touches on a stone fireplace that week, I stood back to admire my work. It was gratifying to know that my own hands had built that. And I was confident that someday I would build something even more impressive.

The Butt Crack Epiphany

Upon returning to my bricklayer job after four months in America, I was laboring high on a scaffold one day, working up quite a sweat, when the weather took a sudden turn—and so did the course of my life.

Here's how I remember it: One moment, the sweat was running in rivulets down my back. Then came the cold snap. The temperature plunged so fast that the sweat was crystalizing at the crack of my butt. And at that very moment, I had an epiphany.

Shivering, I looked around me at the men working with me on the scaffold. Most were in their fifties, and all were feeling miserable—and not just because the weather irritated them. Life irritated them.

I said to myself, "Self, this isn't what's in store for you forever." I didn't know where I was going or how I would get there, but I resolved that I would not wind up miserable like those blokes.

My attitude changed on the spot, and they noticed right away. "So what's got you smiling like a bloody idiot?" one of them asked me.

I held my tongue and continued my work, knowing that I couldn't explain to them the reason for my mood change. I'd realized that this job, these working conditions, were all temporary for me. But it was not for my coworkers and friends.

In the years since, I have relayed that story often. I only do so, though, when I have enough Relationship Equity with people to pull it off. Otherwise, it could sound harsh. They need to know that what I am saying is in their best interests and that I am not just out to put them down.

I told that tale once to a gentleman I had known for some time who was an executive with a major company. He asked to meet me for a beer. For the first twenty minutes, he whined about his situation, which essentially was that he had been knocked down a few pegs in a corporate buyout. He no longer was as big a fish, and this had not done much for his ego.

I listened to him closely until he paused. "So what do you think of all this, Richard?" he asked.

"I think it's sad."

"Yeah, right," he said, "and to make things worse—"

I had to interrupt. "Wait, let me explain. It's not that I don't see how you feel. You had something that you don't have now. I'd be pissed off as well. But there's something else here that's sad." He fell silent. "Listen, let me tell you a story," I said, and I told him about that long-ago day on the scaffold.

"You see, it's all about attitude," I concluded. "You're only going to hurt yourself and everyone around you if your attitude continues to spiral."

He looked a bit shaken, but I could see he was taking my advice to heart. Nobody else had told him what he couldn't see for himself.

"The way I see it," I said, "is that you have a decision to make: figure out what's going to make you happy where you are, or get the hell out and find a job at a different company."

A few months later, he texted me to tell me that he had been promoted to the global CIO at that same company. "And it's because of your butt crack story," he said. He thanked me profusely for telling him what he had needed to hear. He had realized that if he wanted to be happier, he needed to make it happen—and it would start with a change in his attitude. We had built enough equity in our relationship that tough words worked.

The gentleman later told me that he had shared my story with numerous others who found themselves in situations that were similar to what he had experienced. I find it gratifying, if that's the word, to hear that the ice in my butt crack long ago and far away is still an inspiration that has been changing the lives of others to this very day.

It didn't take long for the next opportunity to come my way. One day I took a call from a fella at Camp America, the organization that had sent me to the United States, who had a proposition for me.

"Richard, we got good reports on you, and we'd like you to work as a recruiter for us here in the UK. We want you to go around to college campuses and persuade young people to do what you did and spend a summer as a camp counselor in America."

I don't know whether he even finished the sentence before I responded: "Absolutely!" I was excited at the chance to inspire in others the enthusiasm for travel and adventure that I had felt myself. That summer, I took a busload of my recruits to London for a hiring career fair. I grew up only a couple of hundred miles from London, but it was light-years from the life I had known in Settle. I don't know how many of the recruits were looking wide-eyed at the big city. I know I was.

Opportunities have a way of multiplying once you get in the habit of accepting them. Because I decided to lead the charge down to that job fair, I happened upon another camp owner who offered me a position. So, the following summer, I went back to the States to work at a specialized camp for golf and tennis instruction at Haverford College near Philadelphia in Pennsylvania. This time, when I returned to my bricklayer job, I started to ask myself in earnest the same question that my boss had asked me four years earlier. *Why the hell are you a bricklayer?*

> Opportunities have a way of multiplying once you get in the habit of accepting them.

Never for a moment had I thought that I was cut out to go to college. Still, I decided to visit a career advisor in a nearby town a bit bigger than Settle.

"I'm twenty-two years old," I told her. "It's too late for me, right?" Wrong, she said, and she told me about a "mature student" program in which I could be admitted if I could meet the minimum academic requirements.

I went to night school for a year to fulfill that requirement, and, to my surprise, I was accepted into a prestigious college for physical education. I enjoyed my college years and did well. I finally felt a clear sense of direction. Having been out and about in the world, I felt more motivated to succeed than did some of my younger classmates. I graduated in 1994 at the age of twenty-seven.

All along, others had been seeing something in me that I had not recognized in myself. They opened doors for me, but it was up to me to step through those doors. I might instead have chosen to back away—*no thank you, that's not for me, I don't fit in here.* I took chances, and that made all the difference.

Such was my mindset when I crossed paths with Bill Carr. I was the one who needed to pick his brain, not vice versa. It couldn't have taken him long to see that I really didn't have much of a clue about the business, and yet he looked beyond that. He cared more about potential than accomplishments. He was looking for mettle, not medals.

The People Business

I fell into the information technology field by chance. When I graduated from college, I never expected that I would enter this area. I knew I wanted to spend time in America, having gotten a taste of it in my camp counselor days, and I was proud of my newly acquired degree in physical education. I wanted to teach, but I soon discovered that my credentials obtained in England were not recognized in the States.

I was distraught, to put it mildly, but I was determined to stay on course. Lisa and I were married with a newborn by then and living in Saint Louis to be close to her family. For months, we lived in the basement of her mother's home, and I had taken a construction job while I applied for teaching positions. I made plans to attend night school so that I would be qualified to teach, but with a young and growing family to support, I also looked for other job opportunities.

Now back in those days, folks would pay a quarter for a daily publication called a newspaper, in which they would find classified ads. I looked there. Scanning the columns of ads, I noticed an interesting one that started with four questions in bold letters: "Are you competitive? Are you good with people? Are you not scared of the phone? Do you have basic computer skills?" A company was seeking to fill an open IT position, the ad said.

I looked up from my breakfast plate, puzzled. "Lisa, what does 'IT' mean?" I asked her. I had no idea. But I already had some strong written references by virtue of the variety of connections I had made across the pond. I believe those references are what got me the job. I had figured it might be a good idea to ask my coworkers in the youth service to write down what they thought of me, so I brought those old letters, blotched with White-Out, along with me to the interview. The hiring manager chose to look closely at those and to overlook the obvious shortcomings. He knew I had a lot to learn, but he felt confident that I would and could learn it.

I rushed back to our basement to tell Lisa. "I got the job!" I said. "It's twenty-five thousand a year! And on top of that, I get commissions!" I slowed down, and wrinkles creased my forehead. "Lisa, what's a commission?" It was another concept that I had yet to grasp. I didn't yet know how I would earn my pay as an IT recruiter.

On my first day on the job, my new boss, Dave Hume, assured me that he would be teaching me some things that I would use for the rest of my life—"except they won't work in your marriage," he said with a grin. I grinned back and nodded, pretending that I understood. Frankly, at that point, I still didn't know what IT was all about, or much about my responsibilities, which essentially would be inside sales.

He was so right, though. He taught me questioning techniques. He taught me that people will always answer you, but sometimes you need to ask a lot of follow-up questions to get below the surface, to get the truth on the table. He taught me that much of one's success in a career, and in life, will come from understanding what makes people tick. I had a lot to learn then. And the bit about marriage? He was right about that, too. Unlike in business, I quickly learned that my wife often decides not to answer my questions. Even so, you still are expected to get below the surface, to figure out the various tickings of the heart. I had a lot to learn about marriage, too. Still do.

I owe a debt of gratitude to that man—not only for his wisdom about people but also for sending me to Chicago to open a new office when I scarcely knew what I was doing. He took a chance on me, and because he did, I met Bill Carr. Bill and I saw eye to eye immediately. We shared a perspective that people are the prime factor in the equation of success and that a top qualification must be the quality of the soul, and so we joined forces to create something new. And the rest, as they say, is history.

The people part is why I still am in the IT field today. My company deals with an ever-changing technology that is crucial to our clients' success. I find it gratifying to be able to help them with our specialty. The key word there is *help*. That is what comes first for us. We employ our estimable skills and resources to improve the situation of those who can use our services—as well as the situation of those we send out to do the job.

Long after my boss in Saint Louis gave me his advice for a lifetime, I still am focusing every day on figuring out what makes people tick. I never tire of the dynamics and complexities of human interactions. After all, our business does not have a physical product to sell. What we "sell" is a cadre of smart people with an abundance of tech talent whom we have taught to excel and to serve. We often find excellence in unexpected places and develop it to potential. Our goal is to expand the pool of talent available to our industry.

> Caring about people is central to both good business and good living. That is the foundation of all success—and Relationship Equity is the cornerstone.

For me, though, the fact that our business is IT is secondary to the fact that we can make a difference for people with clear and solvable needs. The only way to do that effectively is to listen intently and ask the right questions. If you do that, they will tell you what is on their minds and what they really want. If you don't, they very well might go somewhere else.

A business needs to make money to survive. That is about as fundamental as it gets. Business is foremost about service, whether you are offering a better widget or a wiser way. In one way or another, it is about improving lives. Caring about people is central to both good business and good living. That is the foundation of all success—and Relationship Equity is the cornerstone.

Why the Hell I Became a Bricklayer

For five years I was a bricklayer, until the age of twenty-one. Never would I have dreamed that one day I would be looking back on the things I learned and applying them to the business world.

One of those stories was why the hell I became a bricklayer in the first place. At age sixteen, my career options were farming, factory, or construction. Those were the expectations for many young men in my little town—expectations that were imposed both by others and by themselves. I had expected to join my dad at the creamery, but I trusted him when he quashed that notion.

So what next? My mother, who was a networking natural, knew the wife of a man who owned a construction company. The interview took thirty seconds and consisted of one question: Did I prefer to work inside or outside? I ventured that I would rather work outside, I suppose, and the boss forthwith designated me an apprentice bricklayer. "You're hired. You can go now," he said, and that was that.

Was it mere happenstance that the construction job into which my mum networked me would open the opportunity to work with my boss at a youth club? Was I simply in the right place at the right time when other offers came my way—to travel to America and to recruit others to do the same? My camp counselor experience changed my life profoundly and forever. I hope some of those whom I recruited would say the same.

Are we all just tossed about by the tides, destined to come ashore who knows where? There is a degree of randomness in our lives. I understand that. Still, to each of us come distinct choices. We can ignore them or maybe flip a coin—or we can choose to respond intentionally. Good luck isn't enough. We must know what to do with that good luck. We need to step forward confidently to embrace opportunities rather than shuffle in shyness and decline them, feeling unworthy. We should ride the waves, not let them sweep us under.

I am where I am because my dad didn't want me to work under the conditions he did and because my mum knew someone who could start me out. And that someone knew others, who knew others. And on it went. At every step, helpful souls introduced me to a world much broader than I had experienced, one that was much brighter than I had imagined. I learned things from them that I could use for a lifetime. I said yes to them. And along the way, I met the woman who finally would say yes to me and become my lifelong love.

People seldom forget it when you go out of your way to be helpful to them, and they will want to repay the kindness in some way, somehow, somewhere down the road. The return is rarely immediate, nor is it guaranteed. But when it happens, it tends to come back in multiples. Can you imagine a world where the modus operandi was taking action to benefit others? As Louis Armstrong sang, "What a wonderful world it would be."

As a small-town boy from the hills of Yorkshire, I was destined to become a man who would overcome limitations and expectations. In time I would discover that my purpose was to help others to change their lives for the better. I was on my way to becoming a man who would explore opportunities and possibilities. I had to begin somewhere, so I started in my hometown among the people I already knew, and I resolved to offer my best and to make the most of whatever came my way.

And that, friends, is why the hell I was a bricklayer.

4

LINKS ON THE LINKS

"I have to tell you, that's the best hat I have ever seen in my life," I recently told a stranger sitting at a bar in Wisconsin. Each year I go on a golf trip with three friends. We stay at a cabin in the woods that is owned by one of the four—Scott White—inspiring my naming it White Castle. After hitting the links, we head out to a tavern or two.

It was in one of those taverns during a recent trip that I sat next to a fella who sported a long silver beard, a patch over his right eye, and a proper white Stetson that would be the envy of any cowboy—and in Wisconsin, no less. He leaned closer, trying to make out my words, and I noticed his hearing aid.

"Your hat," I said a little louder, pointing to it. "Fantastic."

He smiled broadly and extended a hand. "J. C.'s my name," he said, and we struck up a conversation. He introduced me to his wife on the stool next to him, and we swapped a few stories. He was a

Vietnam veteran, he told me, as we shared some highlights of our life journeys.

"This might sound a bit weird," I told him, "but my daughter loves hats like yours. Could I take a picture of the two of us together? I'd like to send it to her." I pulled out my wallet. "In fact, let me give you twenty dollars for the honor."

He wouldn't take the money, nor would he let me buy a round for him and his wife. He was more than pleased, though, to pose for some photos with me, and we chatted a while longer until they had to leave.

"We shall meet again here next year," I vowed, and I added his name to my contacts. And as they were heading out, he turned back and put his hat on the bar. "This is for you," he said, and he wouldn't take no for an answer.

"He's been coming here for fifteen years," Brandy, the bar owner, told me afterward, when I asked her if she had his contact information. "He wears that hat every single time, so for him to give it to you is pretty crazy." And quite an honor. When I returned home, I went hat shopping and mailed him a replacement, somewhat different but, to my eye, just as striking—to which he sent me an exuberant thank-you.

Now that, friends, is the essence of Relationship Equity. A guy walks into a bar, and what happens? He meets a kindred spirit who finds it far more fulfilling to give than to receive. It made his day to make my day. He had no expectation of anything in return, but how could I not reciprocate such generosity?

I had only wanted a picture. Actually, I had only wanted to meet the guy, but I got much more. And I don't mean the hat. I got a new friend. Though I probably will be seeing him but once a year, I am confident that we will pick up each time where we left off.

I enjoy talking to strangers. Meeting people at random isn't unusual for me. When you find people to be fascinating, talking to strangers is easy. I can step into just about any gathering, whether in a pub or at a convention, and in ten minutes I will be chatting with a circle of folks whom I have just met.

That doesn't come naturally to everyone, I know, and for many it is easier to get to know others when doing something together, some activity that is both engaging and that serves as a springboard for conversation.

And that is why God created golf.

The Great Leveler

I have developed countless relationships on the fairways. After all, I never would have met my new friend in Wisconsin had I not been there to play golf. Those relationships have led to other relationships—and not just with golfers, of course. I have found the same sort of camaraderie among fishermen, for example, and football fans. Sports have a way of bonding people.

Golf has been part of my life since my early years. I played on a course near Settle that was on a farm near our home, with electric fences around the greens to keep the sheep and cows away. Once, after I sliced a ball into the pasture, I watched as a cow lumbered over to it, sniffed it, and ate it. I couldn't find a word in the rule books about what to do in such a situation.

Not only golf but rugby and football, too, were a major part of my world as a youth in Northern England. As I got older after moving to America, I no longer participated in the contact sports. ("If you're going to be the breadwinner," my wife advised me, "you probably

41

shouldn't do those things.") To this day, though, when I return to my hometown, I like to spend time with my old teammates.

I have learned through the years that enjoying sports together can be a catalyst for building strong relationships that have the potential of enduring for a lifetime. And golf, far and away, has been foremost among those sports for me. It's all about the people and the game. They are focusing on the game and their fellow players.

Golf is a great leveler. Out on the links, most people aren't thinking about the kind of car you drive or your social status. As you play together, you begin to share your stories—your successes, your wishes, your vulnerabilities. Not everyone plays golf, of course. But whether golfing or fishing or hunting or playing cards, whatever the pastime, what matters most is spending the time together to connect one-on-one and to build the bonds of friendship.

That is a good way to develop solid business relationships as well, so long as you go about it sincerely, not opportunistically. If you develop genuine friendships because you are interested in people, the business opportunities tend to arise over time as you see ways that you can help one another.

Out in the fresh air, though, most of the talk isn't about business at all. Still, as one game leads to another, you sometimes explore other ways you might play well together. When you have experienced together the rigors of a golf course, you can better negotiate the rigors of a business deal. There are bogeys and birdies in both.

Gone Fishing

I never thought of myself as a fisherman, but I have become increasingly interested in the sport since we purchased our home on North Captiva Island in Florida, where fishing is a big part of the culture. In that world, developing a love of fishing just seems natural. You might say it's catching.

I recently had three friends down for a fishing outing, and one of them invited his roommate from his college days who had remained a pal of his. That gentleman, whom I was meeting for the first time, was a high-level IT executive with a major company, and after our introductions and a conversation or two, I realized that the potential was there not only for friendship but also for a business relationship.

The four of us were together for four days. I spoke not a word of business with that fella, but we did engage in a lot of fishing and laughing and storytelling with our fishing mates. And upon our parting, he presented me a gift of an expensive bottle of rum. Jameson is my drink, but I must say rum is fine any time of year.

"When you're back in Minneapolis next week," he said, "let's go get a drink."

"I'd love that," I enthusiastically agreed.

Fast-forward several months, and the two of us sealed a business deal for his company to bring aboard dozens of IT technicians whom my company had trained. A lot happened in between, of course, but consider this: Would that deal ever have happened if we hadn't gone fishing together? Nope. Nor would it have happened if, upon our introduction, I had focused on business first. I would have come across as a phony, an opportunist.

The moral of the story is this: You must focus on what is important, which is authentic relationship development. Regardless of any business outcomes, I gained a great friend that weekend, and that is what matters most of all.

Networking Builds Wealth

Networking is an essential part of building Relationship Equity. A cynic might consider networking to be a calculating use of people for personal gain, but relationships like that would be shallow and devoid of equity with no history of sharing and mutual growth. I'm talking about deeper, lasting relationships that are more than transient and transactional, ones that can enrich your life in ways that are more profound than a bigger bank account.

> When you open yourself up to relationships that expand your world, wealth tends to grow organically.

Yes, I like making money—but making friends matters much more. When you open yourself up to relationships that expand your world, wealth tends to grow organically. Without those meaningful relationships, though, you suffer an immeasurable opportunity cost. You are left to wonder what might have been. When you merely go around adding to a roster of associates, you limit yourself. Those people no doubt have networks of their own, after all, but they are unlikely to share them if you are just some name on a business card.

It has been said that each of us is only six degrees of separation from any other human on the planet. Some call that the six handshakes rule. It is the theory that in our networks of personal acquaintances, we conceivably could meet anyone within six contacts. Imagine the power inherent in that concept. The world could be just a few steps away.

In my network for York Solutions, I feel as if I am at most only one degree of separation away. If I don't know someone in an industry, I probably know somebody who does, and people are aware of those connections because they contact me all the time. Sometimes they ask for an introduction, and sometimes they simply ask whether I would mind if they identified me as their friend. "Not at all," I usually say. I am proud that our company can be of service that way.

If they suggest that I set up a meeting for them, I will do so if I feel confident that there are shared values and a distinct prospect for mutual growth. I value the Relationship Equity that I have built with people and would not want to risk diluting it. I would want the meeting to be a meaningful use of everyone's time because time must be used wisely. It is a precious commodity.

Doing What Comes Naturally

Never would I have imagined, when I was younger, that one day senior executives in the IT industry would seek out my career advice. Helping people figure out their best path is one of the more fulfilling aspects of my own career. I have developed a reputation for helping them think things through.

One such executive, I'll call him Fred, came to me on the recommendation of a peer who is a friend of mine and who knows that I have a multitude of connections in the industry. Fred had been with the same company for nineteen years. Several years earlier, Fred had booted me from his office when I tried to sell him on some of our services. He wouldn't give me the time of day. Now we were face-to-face again, and he wanted my help.

"My executive coach tells me I ought to collaborate more with people outside the company," he explained.

"Sounds like a good idea," I said. "Why don't you?"

"I don't know anybody outside my company. Can you help me?"

It took about three meetings with him before he trusted me enough to open up about what was heaviest on his mind.

"Richard, I'm ready to move on," he said. "I've gone as far as I'm going to go here." It's not easy for an executive who is proud of his accomplishments to admit that. And I understood what he was facing. At his level, you can't just send your résumé through the system. It would go into a black hole. You don't have a chance unless you have connections.

"Okay, let's do this, then," I said. "I can introduce you to executives around town at the places that interest you. First, though, I am hosting an event coming up where you can meet some high-level people. This will be a good starting point for you to let them know who you are and what you can do."

Fred went to the event. After it was over, he approached me. "I can't thank you enough," he said. "I've never been to anything like this before."

"Great, and how many people did you meet with?" I asked.

He smiled sheepishly. "Two," he answered. "And they were both from my own company." We laughed about it. Fred, you're kind of missing the point here, man! But the incident spoke volumes about how hard it can be for some folks to reach out. I was dealing with a brilliant technical mind. I could not do what he does. It doesn't come naturally to me. What I find easy and energizing, he found daunting and draining. The industry needs people with all kinds of skills, and those skills are not often wrapped up in the same package.

Later, after I introduced him to a couple of top executives, he got two job offers. We talked through which offer would be best for him, and he took the job. A few months later, he called me. "Richard, I need to build a large team of IT resources, and I want you to be the exclusive provider."

That is an example of the full life cycle of Relationship Equity and how it has propelled my company's growth. Thanks to Fred, we acquired a huge new client. What had started as a cold encounter has resulted in millions of dollars of new business. Would that have happened if I had not spent a lot of time helping him? Very unlikely. And it never would have happened if I had ushered him out the door the way he had ushered me. That might have been an understandable reaction, but I don't operate that way.

I'm not saying that developing a relationship always produces such lucrative returns. Sometimes we get no reciprocation at all. Or it might take years before the person I have helped is in a position to need our services. You are not going to bat a thousand, but let's say you bat 0.300. A baseball player with that kind of average is one of the best.

The business benefit with Fred arose from a mutual spirit of helpfulness. I expected nothing. This was not a quid pro quo. It was a dividend of a growing friendship and a recognition of shared values. It just came naturally.

Who You Know, How You Know

To some, the prospect of networking is very daunting. It may seem like a stereotype, but I know from experience that many people in the IT world do not take naturally to networking. The field is populated with a large percentage of highly talented, technical-minded introverts. They know a lot. But they do not know a lot of people.

We all have heard the trope that it's who you know, not what you know. Sure, both the *who* and the *what* matter immensely, but what makes it all work is *how* you know. How do you relate to others? How well do you get to know people? Do you regard those you meet as potential friends?

And as for what you know, how are you putting it to good use? Are you advancing your career? What you know won't matter if nobody knows you know it. Whose radar are you on? What have you done to put yourself there? Think about that for a moment, and it will make perfect sense.

I have met many talented people who have yet to embark on a rewarding career path or who feel stuck. Why? For one reason or another, they feel inadequate, as if they cannot measure up to those who seem more educated. Or more privileged. Or more outgoing. They feel like an impostor in a world where they do not belong. They are paralyzed by their own comparisons. That inner voice holds them back from exploring opportunities, and so they stay with what they know. They remain in the world that is familiar to them, and that's fine—until something shakes up that world.

In 2008, their world was shaken. The Great Recession, as it was dubbed, gripped the industry. In such times, the first to go are typically the contractors, and our business caters to the contractors. If they are struggling, we are struggling. To survive, we hunkered down and stayed humble. Everyone in the company took pay cuts. Still, we nearly lost our business, and a lot of our competitors did go under.

I decided during that recessionary summer that one way for people in our industry to cope would be to form a golf networking club. I sent out invitations, including many to IT leaders who had lost their jobs when the economy tanked. Some of them I knew, others I didn't. Many had never looked for a job before; they always had been recruited and had never bothered to make a résumé or set up a LinkedIn profile. They had never been much interested in networking, but now they needed it badly.

Many shared an interest in golf, though, so we all got together regularly that summer. I was strategic about the mixing and matching of the foursomes, hoping to encourage relationships that would help the members of our club with their careers. We were practicing the art of Relationship Equity. As I look back, that was the genesis of the concept that would become central to our company's growth.

The Birth of Think IT

The months passed, and along came the Minnesota winter. No more golf—so now what? One of my associates suggested that we take the Relationship Equity concept indoors and develop it into something more than helping people find jobs. They needed professional development, too. We focused on helping IT leaders in transition find and use the tools for continued success. All along, we were helping talented people prepare for great jobs and introducing them to colleagues who might find value in their services, if not sooner, then later.

As a result, when the market rebounded and many of those folks resumed strong careers as senior leaders, whom do you suppose they called when they needed IT resources? They called us. They knew us. They were comfortable with us. We had helped them with their careers without asking for anything in return, and in gratitude, they chose us as their provider. Business opportunities began to pour in, and we found ourselves bouncing back quickly from those troubling times and leapfrogging most of our competition.

To maintain the momentum, in 2009, we formally created a service within York Solutions that we called the Think IT Association, which we operate to this day. We wanted to do more than just help people who were looking for jobs. We wanted to offer true professional development. In that spirit, we organized events and roundtables and developed a variety of training programs. As I write this, Think IT has over six thousand members on a national basis who are interested in expanding their horizons and collaborating with their peers in the industry. This is Relationship Equity in full swing.

It costs nothing to become a member of Think IT, but it is not free. In some way, you must be willing to give back to the community. You can do that in many ways. You might do a presentation at one of our events, for example, sharing your insights for the benefit of all. Or you might get involved with other development and training programs. (In chapter 7 we will take a close look at one of them, Genesys Works, a training and internship program that York partners with for high school students in underserved communities.)

Think IT is built on the principle of giving and not just taking, and that is what we emphasize to everyone who becomes a member. This is the mindset that fosters the growth of the program and all who join it. The Think IT board of directors has established a written mission to advance professional development through the power of collaboration and networking.

I consider Think IT to be our company's roots, and those roots have continued to grow deeper and wider as they nourish the workforce. The association has helped a wide range of people in our industry to advance their careers. That was an urgent need in recessionary times, and it became an urgent need again during the turbulence of the coronavirus pandemic. To this day, members at all levels of IT leadership gather regularly to put the mission into action.

The birth of Think IT marked the rebirth of York Solutions. It has contributed exponentially to our growth by bringing to our doorstep clients with whom we have built Relationship Equity. As I write this in 2023, we are on track to clear $120 million in annual sales. Through the years our revenue growth has paralleled the growth of Think IT. The correlation has been unmistakable, thanks to the Relationship Equity model that has brought us all our business. As our reputation grew, we advanced from the IT manager level and attracted top executives at major firms. These are people with abundant buying power who need reliable resources, and we are a known entity that they have come to trust. That is what inclines them to say yes to the services that we offer.

The program's booming success testifies to the fact that IT people recognize that networking builds wealth. They might not consider themselves good at it, but they do understand how much they need it. They must reach out and grow if they are to remain relevant in a rapidly changing industry. Networking need not come naturally. It is a skill that can be learned through diligent practice and experience, like golf, for example, or bricklaying, and Think IT is dedicated to teaching it.

Again, our company's financial rebound from near collapse was a dividend of an authentic desire to support our colleagues in the industry. We helped them not only to find good jobs but also to perform at their best in those jobs. We didn't do those things to make money. We made money because we did those things.

> Networking need not come naturally. It is a skill that can be learned through diligent practice and experience.

Friends First, Business Second

"Why don't you get a membership in a golf club somewhere?" my business partner, Bill, suggested at about the time that we were establishing Think IT. I hesitated. Would I fit in there? I still was thinking of myself as a bloke from down on the farm, too blue collar for such highfalutin places. It was my imposter syndrome still lingering. To overcome those thoughts of inferiority, I reminded myself of my father's wisdom: we are all just people, with nobody inherently better than anyone else.

I took Bill's advice, though, and joined the Minneapolis Golf Club, and I fell in love with it. Among the many interesting people I met was an executive of a multibillion-dollar company. While I knew straightaway that we would make great friends, it also occurred to me that York Solutions could be of service to that company.

I considered my approach in developing a relationship with him. To build equity, the motivation must be a desire to connect and help, not simply to rack up a new client, but this gentleman did not need anything from me. He wasn't looking for a job, for example, nor was he in need of any advice so far as I could see. I did not see how I could offer him any value. I also didn't want it to seem that I was only interested in playing with him because of the position he held—it was not about that at all. And I would have been more than okay if our relationship continued to revolve around golf and golf alone. So how does one develop a relationship under such circumstances? Slowly, carefully, intentionally.

What I could share with him was my enthusiasm for golf, so I signed up to play as many rounds as I could with him. Out on the links, we didn't talk much at first. After all, he knew what I did for a living and no doubt expected that I was trying to sell my services to him. I gradually got to know him, though, and he got to know me. I discovered that he was a strong family man. He was dedicated to his work, but his loved ones came first.

I played golf for two years with him, and not once did we talk about work or business. We talked about golf and our families. By increments he got more comfortable with me, and one day he asked me, "Would you tell me a little about your company, Richard?"

Even then, I took it slow. I knew that to do business together, we needed to develop mutual trust. I also knew that I would continue to appreciate our friendship, even if business never entered the equation. In time, though, his company was using our services. Not only that, he calls me sometimes asking for career advice and sometimes just to blow off steam about one thing or another. We have built equity in our relationship. We play golf together, fish together, laugh together. Friendship first, business second. I know no better way.

AWAKENING
TO ONESELF

On a recent trip back home, I happened to be in London on the day they buried the queen. More on that in a moment, but let me pause here to say that after I wrote that last sentence, I started to cross out the words *back home*. After all, I have lived happily in America for most of my life. I left the words as they were, though, and why? Because my roots are over there, across the pond, and so is a big chunk of my heart. If that doesn't define "home," what does?

In the days after Queen Elizabeth died at age ninety-six, I began getting a stream of notes and texts from acquaintances, some of whom I hadn't seen in years. "Sorry for the loss of your queen," they wrote, as if they figured I'd had tea with her daily. Though it has been three decades and more since I traversed the pond, it would appear that I am eternally British. No doubt it is my accent that leads people to dub me a loyal subject of the crown.

I am loyal to my roots, for sure. I bear my accent proudly as an emblem of my past—and one's past informs all the days of one's life, for better or for worse. To this day I am proud of the part of me who still is that bricklaying farm lad from the town of Settle. My Northern England upbringing shaped me, in many ways, into the person I am today—but I did not let it narrow my expectations. The world was too wide and opportunities too vast for me to settle for what Settle had to offer me. I would miss the hills that raised me, the family and friends who supported me, but I knew that I could build more for myself than chimneys and stone walls. The spirit of adventure had me in its grasp.

I did feel self-conscious and awkward about my identity at times during my early stints in America. On my second trip there, for example, when I was teaching golf at a summer camp near Philadelphia, a lot of the kids came in from Boston. They would say such things as "Hey, Richahd, whehh should we pahk the cahh?" I did not yet recognize that was the Bostonian way of talking. I thought it was the Bostonian way of mocking me, since I tend to overlook the *R*s, too.

Those trips to America marked a turning point in my life, just as it was a turning point when my boss asked me if I would replace him as youth leader so he could retire. I was honored to be chosen, especially because they had to adjust the policy regarding age so that I could take the position. I was nineteen years old at the time, and the previous minimum age was twenty-one. There was zero hesitation that it was what I would do. It was because of that offer that I got the opportunity to come to the US—and every opportunity since, for that matter.

One thing leads to the next might seem like a silly old saying that states the obvious, but it sums up the connectedness of different points in our lives. There is a catch, though. Nothing leads anywhere unless you act on it. If you shrug, your world shrinks.

I chose not to shrug.

"I Like Your Accent!"

Though I have had some reservations about my Yorkshire accent in the past, I have grown to become quite proud of it. I have admittedly lost a bit of it over the years, but it comes swiftly back whenever I go home. My American family notices the subtle changes every time. In fact, they have said that my accent bounces back instantaneously as soon as I answer a phone call from an English caller.

I have always been fascinated by accents and the way that most of us tend to draw conclusions about people based on the way they talk—subconsciously or not. For example, when the dialect of my hometown is heard in England, the speaker is immediately considered to be of the blue-collar, hardworking class.

In England, people categorize you by your accent. Mine, for example, designates me a farmer. I may as well have had the word *farmer* branded on my forehead. People know straightaway where I grew up—"a proper Yorkshire lad," they might say. As the saying goes, "Yorkshire born, Yorkshire bred. Strong in the arm, thick in the head." As far as I'm concerned, that is not too far away from the truth.

It did, however, give me some pause when I thought about coming to America. I was worried that my way of speaking would bring along the usual line of judgmental assumptions about social class.

What I didn't know to expect was that there *would* be assumptions about me because of the way that I spoke, just in an entirely different way. I would say eight out of ten Americans first guess that I am an Australian, perhaps because I'm a big, dumb-looking blond guy with a foreign accent. They just can't distinguish how we talk—even though, to my ears, the Aussie dialect is as different from mine as Scottish is from South African. If you don't know what I'm talking about, I suggest you Google a sample of both accents, because it is hard to believe that they are speaking the same language.

I still find it bewildering that many Americans assume a certain level of intelligence whenever they hear an English accent. I'm not sure if this is associated with movies or TV shows they may have watched, or if it is just a subconscious assumption, but it is a common occurrence in conversations that I have had.

And many Americans think accents are something only other countries have. One day at the market, a girl about twelve years old heard me talking to the checkout clerk. She and her mum were behind me in line.

"I like your accent!" she said brightly.

"And I like yours," I responded just as brightly. She looked puzzled.

"But—I don't have an accent," she said.

"Really?" I said, smiling. "Australians have accents, don't they?" She agreed. "And then there's Scottish, and French, and German—those are all accents, right?" She nodded. "So here in America, what accent do you have?"

"Americans don't have accents," she said resolutely. "They just don't."

It's not unusual to hear that perspective in a land where dialects don't seem to change for hundreds of miles.

Shortly before we married, Lisa and I went to Disney World, where I could pick out an array of British accents among the many foreigners visiting there. I heard Liverpool and Newcastle—and "yeah, that one is definitely Birmingham," I told her. Even within short distances, there are nuances. I went to a high school on the border of North Yorkshire and

Lancashire, and the kids always knew who was from where just by their manner of speech.

I find it refreshing that Americans, such as that girl in the market, don't make such judgments. They might not know whether I'm an Aussie, Scottish, Welsh, or whatever, but no matter—they just know they like what they are hearing.

Wake Up, Little Suzie

It's not as if I was walking boldly into some bright light, though. I had my doubts. For one thing, I applied late to the Camp America program that would take me overseas for the summer of 1988. The other applicants mostly were European university students who were a couple of years younger than me, but I presumed they were smarter, by definition. They had a long summer to fill up. I didn't. I was spending my days building fireplaces, converting stone barns into homes, and figuring out whether this venture was worth the risk of losing my steady employment.

I worked out the details, the weeks turned to days, and soon I found myself on a charter flight with an assortment of young people bound for summer camps across the United States. When we landed in New York, it felt as if I had landed on the moon and that I was an English version of Crocodile Dundee, minus the knife. I had no idea what state I'd end up in—nobody had told me yet—but figured I would know soon enough. And like Mick Dundee, I talked to everybody I came across on those busy New York streets. Funnily enough, not many people wanted to engage in conversation with the foreigner in the loud outfit, walking around like a Martian that had just landed on a new planet.

We had four hours to kill before the buses picked us up.

Time for a pint, I thought, and looked around the airport for anything that resembled a pub. Down the corridor I saw a promising destination and joined the queue there—or rather, the throng. Americans tend to converge.

"I'd like a pint of Guinness, please," I said to the young lady at the counter when my turn came, then squinted at the lighted menu on the wall behind her. I figured I could down me a pint while I decided on my sandwich. I've never been one to eat on an empty stomach.

"Could I see your ID, please?"

"Wha—my ID?" Why did she want to know my name? "I'm Richard!" I offered. "You?"

She sighed. "Your ID, or no beer."

Let me point out that I had been drinking in pubs in England since I was sixteen years old. That wasn't uncommon where I grew up, and nobody ever questioned me. Nobody cared—until now, and I didn't care for the way she cared.

"Why?" I asked. A reasonable question. Sure, I was twenty-one, but why did I need to prove it?

She looked at me as if I were from Pluto and rolled her eyes. "Next in line!" she called out.

And then I said it: "You cheeky cow!"

She was doing her job, and I called her a cheeky cow. Those words came out of my mouth.

Now, in my defense, let me explain that when you call somebody a cow in England, the word carries no connotation regarding one's bodily dimensions or quality of countenance. I was suggesting only that this lass was a bit annoying, not that she was unappealing. And cheeky is kind of endearing, right? Sort of like saucy? Or maybe spirited?

Looking back now, I can only laugh while imagining what she must have said to her friends about that interaction or how she described me.

This was my first taste of the subtle cultural difference between a small farming town in Northern England and the biggest city in this land of opportunity called the United States. To the American ear, I had called her fat, ugly, and bitchy. She was unimpressed.

I headed to the toilet, and as I stood there doing what one does, I felt somehow inspired to hum a tune and sing a few words of it: "Wake up, little Suzie, wake up … we gotta go home!" Maybe it was random, or maybe I was having some misgivings about leaving the people and places I knew. *No turning back now*, I thought.

Then I heard a voice that wasn't mine singing in harmony. I zipped up and turned to see a friendly face at the sink combing his hair. We had been on the same flight. Our eyes met in the mirror, and he smiled broadly at me.

"My name's Rob," he said, and I introduced myself. "Let me grab my guitar," he said.

Returning to our group, he tuned and strummed and burst out into a Beatles song—and we all sang along to it, and then another, and another. A crowd formed around us, joining in. Was it minutes or hours? I lost track of time—and then I noticed the TV cameras. We made the news that night. (I would later be surprised to bump into Rob again back in England when I finally went to college. He was a senior at the same school.)

I stepped away from the revelry to find a phone booth so I could tell my parents that I had landed safe and sound.

"Richard, there's a letter here for you," my dad said. "It came in the post after you left. It says congratulations, you are going to Decatur, Michigan, to be a camp counselor and teach golf." I had never heard of Michigan, but Dad said the letter mentioned something about a lake there.

"Sounds good," I said.

Soon I was on a train to Kalamazoo and onward to my destination. The camp was beautiful and had a pond for swimming and boating. The camp owner showed me around, and I thanked him profusely for this opportunity.

"And I love your Lake Michigan," I said. He burst out laughing and took me to his office where he pointed to a map.

"Do you see this big blue expanse up here?" he said. "That there is Lake Michigan. And see this tiny dot down here? That's my pond."

I felt confused and puzzled. I had never heard of the Great Lakes before! Now, as I recall that scene, I can only smile at the young and naive lad that I once was.

It wasn't long, though, before I beheld Lake Michigan with my own eyes. On our first day off from camp duties, we headed up to South Haven. I had befriended a fellow counselor named Gene, who was from a small town in Nebraska. We watched the yachts crossing the harbor.

"Ever been in a boat like that?" I asked my new buddy.

"No. You?"

"Gene, I've never even seen a *boat* before, let alone a yacht," I said, rising to wave exuberantly at the next yacht passing. I could see hands waving back.

"Hey, you out there!" I called out across the water. "Give us a ride!"

Gene quickly caught my spirit and joined in. "Give us a ride!" we shouted together, even louder. "Pick us up!" And—wouldn't you know—they did?

We spent that whole afternoon cruising out on the Big Sea Water, as the Native Americans called it—and indeed it seemed as wide as the ocean I had crossed only days earlier. I jumped in and got a mouthful of that water. *A sea without salt? How could this be?*

More surprises awaited me. I was a young man with a buoyant spirit determined to find adventure in this new world so different from anything that I had known.

Little did I know what was to come ...

On the Playing Field

Among the counselors at that camp were only two foreigners—an Australian lad and me. The others all were Americans from parts as unknown to me as the land down under. During that first week before the kids arrived, the emphasis was on getting to know one another and bonding. We all gathered in a big circle for introductions, about thirty of us, including the camp owners.

I listened as each took a turn, and it seemed they all started out by naming their college and major. They either had just graduated or were in their senior year, and all declared how much they were looking forward to this summer job. College clearly was central to their identity, but I had never heard of any of the ones they mentioned. I didn't even know what a "major" *was.*

Then it was my turn. I was the last one.

"Hello. My name is Richard Walker. I'm from a small town in Northern England called Settle. And I'm a bricklayer."

First came a snort or two and then laughter burst out all around the circle. Were they expecting me to say that I was just kidding and then wow them with my academic credentials? I hadn't yet given a thought to going to college. I didn't think it was even remotely possible for me. These kids had been places and accomplished things—*and me?* I felt about as important as an empty pint of Guinness. This was my first real encounter with imposter syndrome.

As the weeks passed, though, I realized that none of them really cared who had gone to which college. It didn't come up again. As we got to know one another, what mattered most was how we worked together and how the kids responded to us. Nothing else.

I soon realized that I had something to offer. I didn't have a degree, but I had been out in the world longer than the others, and I already knew a thing or two about working with kids. Now these ones were very different from the rural farm kids I had known, but I was still able to find ways to relate to them. I quickly realized that kids were kids, whether they were from affluent American families or humble farming backgrounds. I had value, and the others could see it even when I could not.

In the beginning, I believe that the kids migrated toward me because I was a novelty. I spoke differently, I acted differently, and they were fascinated by it. I saw the importance of making them laugh and showing them that not everything needs to be taken too seriously. But that would only take me so far.

As they were curious about me, I was equally fascinated with them and the way that they lived. It was so foreign to the way I always had. Because of this, I felt inspired to ask them questions that I am not sure the other leaders did. I was too curious to resist, and the bonds that we formed seemed to be stronger because of it.

For the summer finale, my fellow counselors and the campers together chose me as a team leader. Two people, out of the collective thirty, were chosen to recognize their hard work and their ability to inspire the kids. It was a proud moment for me, one that made me realize that they appreciated who I was and what I could contribute regardless of my lack of a formal education. Perhaps I wasn't an impostor after all.

The relationships we forged during that summer of 1988 were powerful, and I am still in touch with some of those folks today, namely my good friend Gene. The experience was an awakening for me. My confidence in myself grew tremendously once I realized that I had something unique to bring to the table. Those other counselors were not better than me, despite their university pedigrees. And I was not better than them, despite my prior experience.

What we learned that summer was how to succeed by functioning as a team. We had been sent out to the same playing field. For the betterment of all, we would need to combine our various skills. Each of us was learning that as much as those skills mattered, it would be the strength of our relationships and working together cooperatively that would stay with us.

Life Worth Living

That summer marked my coming of age. I was developing a far better sense of self-awareness. All young people go through a similar metamorphosis. Their questions are elemental: *Who am I? What do I stand for? What will be my values? What impact will I have on this world?* They gravitate toward role models to emulate, some of them good ones and others, well … questionable. They explore a variety of identities and try them on for size.

All in all, it is a healthy part of growing up. As those young people mature, they presumably become better able to reconcile their values with their behaviors. They go on to pursue productive and authentic lives.

Quite often, though, something disrupts that natural growth. It might be cultural or economic demands. It might be family pressures. Or it simply might be the voices in their head saying, *I can't do that* or *I'm not smart enough* or *it's just too late for me.* Limiting themselves before they start, they end up toiling for years in jobs and careers that others might believe are appropriate for them but that bring them little satisfaction. They get stuck and can't see a way out.

From where I'm sitting, this seems to be much more prevalent with today's youth. It is indisputable that technology has changed the constructs of society since I arrived in America in 1988. Back then, if you wanted someone's opinion, you would need a quarter and their phone number on hand. Not even the movie *Back to the Future* could predict that the youth of today would own a hand-held device that can not only communicate with the whole world but also can tell you anything you want to know in a split second.

There is so much more happening in the background at any given second now than there was back then; technology and social media have made it so that these questions of doubt are no longer only internal. In addition to your own self-doubt, there are now societal pressures influenced by social media that can have a profound negative impact on the psyche of today's youth.

> It is how you respond that is what matters most. We are all in control of how we respond to any source of information.

But, like anything else, it is how you respond that is what matters most. We are all in control of how we respond to any source of information.

My summer overseas helped me gain the traction that I needed. It helped me to dispel the limits that I had been placing on myself. I was discovering that I could define myself and my own dreams, whatever those might be, rather than just falling in line with what I imagined was my destiny. I felt confident that I could hold my own in whatever circles I chose to move.

That confidence would ebb and flow, of course, in the months and years ahead. I grew, but growth comes in spurts. I still had a lot to discover about myself, but I did know this: I was not some impostor or great pretender who should lie low. Instead, I was eager to meet as many people as possible. I still had no idea what I was going to do with my life. The prospect of higher education still seemed far-fetched for someone like me. But I was *me*. I knew—win or lose—that I had the power to choose which direction my life would go.

> I have seen firsthand what you can achieve once you recognize your own value and gain the confidence to move forward.

A wise old Greek fella named Socrates summed it up in two words: "Know thyself." That is what makes your life worth living, he said. By taking a close look at myself, I was finally able to see that I had potential greater than I had presumed.

So why have I only been talking about myself and my experiences so far in this book? Because I understand what it is like to feel stuck. I can empathize with those who feel that they don't fit in or don't hold value outside of the job they've found themselves in. And I have seen firsthand what you can achieve once you recognize your own value and gain the confidence to move forward.

I know this, as well: There are many others out there who need to break free from the constraints into which others have placed them or in which they have placed themselves. Way too often, people allow others to stamp out their destiny. They buy into a crippling belief that they cannot aspire to more, and they feel like outsiders among people whom they presume to be better than they are.

They aren't better, I want to shout. Each of us possesses, in some way, a skill or a talent that is essential to the success of the team, whatever that team might be. Those abilities may not be readily apparent because they have been lying dormant. Our society cannot afford to overlook those talents any longer. It is well past time we wake them up.

A Heart to Help

Our mission at York Solutions is to tap into those possibilities and provide opportunities to excel. My associates in the IT industry generally would agree that it is increasingly difficult to find qualified employees. The demand for them is growing rapidly, and institutions of higher education have been scrambling to produce enough young graduates to fill the entry-level jobs.

It's time to expand the search for talent—and at York, we are finding it in places where most companies have seldom looked. People with the right skills are living and working all around us in our communities at jobs that are not the best fit for them. Some are working in warehouses or supermarkets or factories. Others are working in hospitals or law offices or pharmacies. Some are earning far less than their potential. Others are doing just fine as far as salary goes—but not so fine when it comes to professional satisfaction.

The majority of them are not kids. They have been around the block a few times, so to speak, and they possess life skills and people skills that can only be attained with life's experiences and that make big impacts on a working team. They are smart, motivated, and eager to make something more of themselves—if only somebody would reach out to them, encourage them, and develop their innate abilities. Sometimes it is even as simple as a door being opened, and their true talents will come through.

I know how it feels to be aching to break free of limitations. I have been blessed to cross paths with people who helped me develop new strengths and overcome weaknesses. Without the support of those who met me at every step, I might never have built the confidence that I needed to thrive. If I hadn't taken pride in my roots, I'd probably still be that boy who was self-conscious about talking like a northerner. I might have remained as I was, working hard but feeling small.

Life can get comfortable, like an old pair of shoes. Sometimes people stay with what they know rather than risk the unknown—but without a sense of adventure, they also risk stagnation. Better to break in some new shoes and get moving. You can always go home again. I know. I ventured out and learned more about myself, but I never forgot who I was, and I never will. In my mind I am still that Crocodile Dundee from England that I was in 1988.

Out of gratitude, I wish to pay it forward. To all who have helped me grow in self-awareness, I want to say thank you. And I will do this by passing it on, by helping others to do the same so that they might also redirect their careers and their lives. My mission—you could call it an obsession some days—is to offer such opportunities to those who otherwise might hesitate to take the first steps toward something new and exciting.

My colleagues at York Solutions share that same commitment. It is central to our culture and to our business model. Our aim is to build a bigger and better pool of IT talent in a way that will improve people's lives—and in the next chapter, I will explain how we are doing just that.

The Greatest Asset

In the early days of York Solutions, when we were pitching our services, I mostly limited myself to calling on IT managers. In most companies that is the lowest level of leadership, as there are several layers of IT leaders before you get to the C-suite.

Why didn't I aim higher? I did not feel that we, as a company, had enough value to seek out the players on the top rungs of the ladder. What would we be able to offer them? That self-limiting mindset changed dramatically in 2008 and 2009 when we developed Think IT, as I described in the previous chapter. It was not just the IT managers who were looking for jobs as a result of the economic downturn. All levels of leadership were coming to us for help, including the C-suite.

I soon realized that there was an opportunity there—we could offer them value by demonstrating how to effectively network. For many IT professionals, networking does not come naturally. In fact, it can be quite painful.

We got to know one another as people, not as titles, and formed relationships that extended further than talking numbers and projections. Before long, I was hearing directly from CIOs who wanted to meet with me one-on-one. As we began assisting the top-level executives, we also were opening our prospects of selling our services to them. Those relationships have continued to expand through the years.

I recently met yet another of those top executives when he filled an opening in a foursome at our shared golf club.

"I've been hoping to play golf with you for at least a year," he told me as we played the back nine. "I hear you're the guy who people should get to know."

"Why didn't you just reach out to me?" I asked him.

"I didn't feel like I should impose," he said.

This encounter was a great reminder of how dramatically things had changed.

In the early days, I felt that I lacked the value needed to associate with high-ranking IT leaders. I thought that my involvement would just be an imposition to them. And here they were, seeking *me* out, worrying about imposing on me. Before we even shook hands, this gentleman believed in me. Word gets around. He'd heard testimonials of how York Solutions helped others with their careers, and he wanted to be part of that scene.

Confidence generates confidence. It can be your greatest asset. I learned that at a summer camp long ago, and I still see it ringing true every day. It also is true that failure can generate failure—and it is that fear that holds people back from the possibility of success. The trick is to define a setback as a lesson learned, not as a failure.

In my time, I have opened several offices, and some of them did not work out. Why? Because I made mistakes—but I have not let those mistakes erode my confidence. Instead, as my colleagues and I contemplate more offices and greater growth, we can face the future feeling more prepared for success than ever before.

Whenever I encounter an opportunity in life, I don't spend undue time wrestling with whether I could succeed or fail. History has shown me time and time again that if I continue to say yes more often than no, good things will come from it. This has been my approach since that first yes to Camp America, and it forever will be so.

One must weigh risks, of course, but never to the point of paralysis. Instead, say yes to the adventure and stop viewing new endeavors as potential failures. View them as what they are—an opportunity for growth. *Success* and *failure* are relative terms. You can shape them into your own narrative and always find a lesson to take away.

BREAKING DOWN THE BARRIERS

I have a confession to make: I'm about as technical as a pint of Guinness.

I do not fit the stereotype of an "IT guy." It can be a struggle for me to turn on my computer in the morning. I appreciate technology, of course, and have devoted my career to advancing it—yet I still have to ask my kids to help me get Netflix going.

Developing relationships, though, is what comes naturally to me. I like to be out and about, making conversation with people I don't know. I genuinely look forward to meeting people and making friends but, more importantly, to keeping in touch. That is not how most people would describe the typical IT guy or gal. They are often seen as lone wolves.

The *geek* stereotype is unfortunate but not always inaccurate. I have met plenty of people in my field whose concept of networking lies solely in the digital realm. Generally speaking, techies don't tend to be talkers. They are technically brilliant, and sometimes this translates into a different kind of social interaction. Most people lie somewhere between the extremes, of course, but I can say with confidence that the IT world as a whole is weighted more toward the introverted end of the continuum.

Our industry needs both types. We need those smart analytical minds, and we also need people who are adept at making connections and zeroing in on the needs and wants of individuals and the marketplace. One part is not possible without the other, and together they can come up with the best IT solutions.

Most IT leaders would agree, though, that it has become increasingly hard to find qualified technical talent. The traditional place to locate it has been on college campuses. The problem we have found, though, is that everyone is fishing in that same pond—and the resources are dwindling as the demand continues to grow.

In a 2021 survey by Gartner Inc., IT executives identified the lack of available talent as the biggest barrier to adopting new technologies.[2] At the same time, a poll of twelve hundred tech and IT workers, published by TalentLMS and software company Workable, found that 72 percent of them were considering quitting or exploring other job opportunities within the year.[3]

---

2   Gartner, "Gartner Survey Reveals Talent Shortages as Biggest Barrier to Emerging Technologies Adoption," September 2021, accessed April 12, 2023, https://www.gartner.com/en/newsroom/press-releases/2021-09-13-gartner-survey-reveals-talent-shortages-as-biggest-barrier-to-emerging-technologies-adoption.

3   Eric Panselina, Ana Casic, and Keith Mackenzie, "Retaining Tech Employees in the Era of the Great Resignation," Talent MLS, August 2021, accessed April 12, 2023, https://www.talentlms.com/tech-employees-great-resignation-statistics.

Meanwhile, the pool of college graduates will be getting increasingly smaller, according to projections.[4] A college degree, whether in information technology, computer science, or engineering of some sort, is the traditional path to enter the industry. Students do their internship, get that piece of paper, and they are in. In recent years, though, the US college system has been producing too few graduates with the credentials to meet the rising demand.

At the same time, a college diploma is becoming less and less crucial to having a career in IT. Don't get me wrong—a degree is a major accomplishment, and many companies still require one for entry-level positions and further promotions. The good news is that things are changing. The more innovative companies focus less on credentials and more on evaluating a person's technical acuity and ability to learn new concepts.

Many companies, frustrated in their search for talent, have gone overseas to locate what they cannot find in their own backyard. As one door begins to close, they look for another that is opening. In our global economy, technology connects people who live thousands of miles apart as if they were next-door neighbors. Companies are no longer limited to hiring only people who are willing to reside within commuting distance to the office.

The shortage of candidates has worsened in the wake of the coronavirus pandemic, during which many IT employees got their first taste of working remotely—and discovered that they liked it. When major corporations decided that it was time for their people to come back to the office, a lot of those folks decided to go elsewhere, or even get out of the field entirely, so that they could continue working from

---

4   Olivia Sanchez, "With Student Pool Shrinking, Some Predict a
     Grim Year of College Closings," The Hechinger Report, January
     2023, accessed April 12, 2023, https://hechingerreport.org/
     with-student-pool-shrinking-some-predict-a-grim-year-of-college-closings.

home. Attrition in the COVID-19 era has caused massive disruption and turmoil in the industry.

Although those trends have been troubling for the countless companies in need of IT talent, businesses such as ours—that focus on finding and providing that talent—have in turn found opportunities for innovation and growth. More clients have come knocking in search of IT staff and services. They are seeking the help of relationship specialists who can make connections in the IT marketplace.

At York Solutions, our core business model is consulting and contracting. In short, we provide full-blown project delivery services and teams of IT professionals to companies that need IT expertise. We find and train qualified technicians who become our W-2 employees. We then send our people out to the companies that contract with us for our services.

The IT landscape has changed drastically in recent years. As I write this, well into the third decade of the twenty-first century, the imbalance between supply and demand is the worst that I've ever seen, and it appears that it will not be getting better any time soon unless something major changes. Industry leaders must plant the seeds now to grow a talent pool large enough to meet that demand. The winners will be the companies that use innovative ways to attract and retain the top talent.

The Stars Waiting to Shine

In the world of business, stronger relationship skills enhance the chance of success. A prime example of this in my own career was during the Great Recession. During this time, I organized golf outings with the intention of helping laid-off executives connect with new opportunities. Our aim was to build the skills and resources needed to advance a career, and for some of those executives, the push to network was a new concept. But as time went on and they gained confidence in their ability to develop relationships and build equity with them, many of those executives went on to bigger and better things.

The lack of so-called people skills has been seen to hold some individuals back from getting into the field in the first place, even though they might be ideal candidates otherwise. You are unlikely to advance very far if you are not willing to go out, actively looking for opportunities. The bottom line, though, is how you respond once you *find* those opportunities.

In the world of business, stronger relationship skills enhance the chance of success.

A relationship deficit, however, is far from the only reason that some people with the skill set to succeed do not get into the field and build a strong career. More often than not, the reason is simply an education deficit. They do not gain the entry-level skills necessary for their first job. Sometimes they get sidetracked into a field of study that isn't suited for them. Sometimes, for a multitude of reasons, they have an aversion to the typical path of classroom study. Mostly, though, they don't pursue higher education because it is financially unattainable. This subset of the population makes up a large part of what I refer to as the socioeconomic pyramid.

The peak of that pyramid represents wealthy families whose children have a high probability of attending a four-year college. At the base of the pyramid are families for whom that expense is out of reach or nearly so. The distribution of ability, however, is arguably the same from the top to the bottom of that pyramid. Wealth produces opportunities, but it does not increase brain power or problem-solving skills.

SOCIOECONOMIC PYRAMID

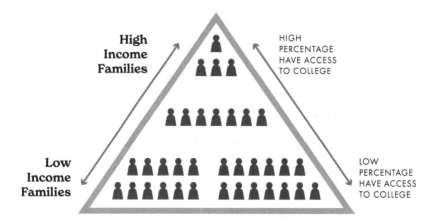

High Income Families

HIGH PERCENTAGE HAVE ACCESS TO COLLEGE

Low Income Families

LOW PERCENTAGE HAVE ACCESS TO COLLEGE

The implication is clear: our society has a broad base of untapped talent. At York Solutions, we are mining for the diamonds in the rough at the base of the pyramid. We have proven that we can transform people with raw ability into valuable employees eager to get to work. They are stars that have been waiting to shine.

A Gold Mine of Talent

The Barriers to Entry program (or B2E for short) that York has developed provides the training needed to begin lifelong careers in IT. It changes lives, putting people and their families on a path to a livelihood that they might never have dreamed possible. I am proud that we have opened this door for them—and the proof is in the pudding. Our B2E program has discovered a gold mine of untapped talent.

The program also is addressing the IT talent shortage. We are creating an alternative pool of employees who are eager to prove their worth. These people have a drive to excel and are often more urgently motivated than their counterparts who hold degrees, making them invaluable to any team they join. The program is life-changing for the individuals, and it is game-changing for the industry. It's the most impactful thing I've ever been involved with in business by far, and it will be an even bigger part of what our company will be doing going forward.

As we began considering how we might tear down some of the barriers that block entry into the industry, we looked at the range of obstacles at play. So many people, for one reason or another, experience interruptions to their careers. A classic example is the mother who takes time off to raise a family but eventually wants to get back into the working world. Or the veteran who spent time in service to their country but after discharge wonders how to readjust to civilian life. And for many others, it's not a matter of the career being interrupted but rather never getting *started*. They labor for years—collecting their weekly pay in unfulfilling jobs, feeling trapped by life's endless obligations and wondering if their big break will ever come.

I felt it was high time that York Solutions developed programs to help people like that get a foothold in the IT industry. One of our first initiatives, which we started in 2017, was designed to offer opportunities in the business side of the IT industry. We looked for candidates with strong interpersonal skills who would be a good fit and introduced them to project management and scrum master roles. Once we identified those who had the right skill set, we hired them right away and rolled them into a training program, at our expense. More than five hundred people went through that program, and we considered it quite a success.

It wasn't enough, though. I kept hearing the same message from some of our bigger clients: *We like what you're doing, but what we need most are the highly technical skills. We need software engineers.* That had been our intention all along, but we knew that meeting that demand would be a heavier lift. It would require a much longer and more involved training program. Such a program would be far more intensive than teaching management and organizational skills. This was a different ball game altogether.

We committed to the concept in 2021 and launched the B2E tech track program, offering comprehensive training for people with an IT aptitude that had gone unexpressed. The applications poured in. We got the word out through community-based groups, and interest spread by word of mouth.

I found it mind-boggling how many people out there have the desire to enter the IT field but aren't able to get a foot in the door. As with our management training program, we identified the applicants who would be a good fit, hired them, and trained them—but for these people, the training would continue once they were placed, depending on the complexity of the technology involved. For this program, though, the issue of finding the right talent was a more complicated one. In order for a candidate to succeed in one of these roles, they need to prove that they have something that cannot be taught—a naturally technical mind and an acuity to learn complex technological concepts. To be able to determine this one fact with a high degree of certainty, we contracted a company that had developed the technology necessary to do so. They spent years perfecting a service that tests the inner workings of one's thought processes, and the model worked so well that we decided to buy the company.

The training that this program offers is a major commitment. Not only for our company but also for every individual considering whether to apply. Despite its ability to launch people into a career of their dreams, they often hesitate to take advantage of the opportunity. If they are depending on a paycheck to support themselves or a family, they may be hesitant to quit a secure job and forgo a certain salary, even though the training program is a paid position. They are facing the prospect of earning a living by doing something entirely different, which brings with it a lot of unknowns. The unfamiliar can be intimidating. For a lot of people, it feels like too much of a risk and too far outside their comfort zone. They worry that they will be stepping into a situation where they will be out of place—where they will not fit in.

Upward of three thousand people applied for the B2E program in its first year. The test that must be passed to gain entry to the program screens for innate tech ability. It doesn't measure how much you know about IT or look at your level of experience and education. Instead, it is concerned with how you process information and how well you critically think. The point of the assessment is not to find out what you have done but rather what you are capable of doing.

The screening test starts out easy but becomes progressively more difficult as it assesses technical acuity. During the test, the applicant is taught how to code and how to use it and then asked to apply it to a problem. They create solutions based on the information that was provided. It isn't a two-hour exam. It continues over the course of two weeks, as they build something from scratch based on what they have just been taught. The lengthiness of the test is by design so that we can assess the candidate's willingness and dedication.

We want to be sure that we are setting the candidates up for workplace success, so only a small percentage of the applicants are accepted into the program. At first it was five out of one hundred, but soon that percentage was rising to eight out of one hundred, as applicants told their like-minded friends about this unique opportunity. And companies interested in developing a more diverse workplace also will be interested in knowing that upward of 70 percent of those in the program are considered to be diverse candidates in the corporate sense.

Even though I know the exact way the test works, I can say with a 100 percent degree of certainty that I would not pass it. My mind just doesn't work that way. Most of my colleagues in IT leadership positions probably would concede that they are not as technically skilled as many of those they hire. That's because our primary job is managing people, and that takes a different touch. That being said, as I have told every single person who has been accepted into this program, I have a great deal of respect for the skills that they have and the way that their brains function. They all have brilliant minds.

Tech work is not for everyone. I advised a friend who wanted to apply to our B2E program and who is a very smart woman, just not in the most technical way. "You have a wonderfully artsy, creative mind," I told her, "but this exam looks for people who think mostly with the other side of the brain." She took the test—and told me afterward that I had been right; it wasn't for her. "But my sister took the test and she passed! *She* can't even draw a stick figure, so I guess we both have our strengths," she added. Her sister joined York in a software engineer position working remotely full-time.

My contributions lie in helping those with technical savvy find their way into lucrative jobs and satisfying careers that they otherwise might never have found. Many would have stayed buried at the bottom of the pyramid. It is my role as a connector that I personally find the most satisfying. Helping others is what I do, and a big part of that is getting folks into the right professional relationships to better chart their course.

Changing Lives

The fella was nearly in tears, and I could see the gratitude in his eyes. "I didn't expect to get into this program," he told me, "but I knew I couldn't go on the way I was." He told me that he had been laboring eighteen hours a day trying to support his family but was barely able to make ends meet. "Something had to change," he said.

"That's right," I said. "And what's about to change is your life."

We have seen a lot of people like him enter our Barriers to Entry program. It has brought new beginnings for people from a wide variety of backgrounds. Most of them had been holding down jobs, often physically demanding ones.

"I thought I'd give this program a shot," a warehouse worker told me after we selected him, "because I had nothing to lose," he said. Others were landscapers and construction workers. We have found a lot of talent in the blue-collar world among people who never had the chance to go down a different career path. And for every one person we find, you can be sure that there are countless others who have yet to be discovered.

I recently spoke with an applicant who seemed mildly embarrassed about his background, as if it were something he should hide. "Believe me, I can relate, mate," I told him, "because I was that way myself for years, coming from farming and construction. I didn't want people to know. And then one day I decided that it was only me who could decide who I would be. My past didn't define me; it strengthened me, because I understood we all deserve to be treated the same. I wanted to give myself, and everyone else, a chance."

That's what we are doing with our B2E program. We are giving a chance to people who may have spent years doubting themselves and feeling stuck. No matter their background, it shouldn't limit what they are able to accomplish. Many of the B2E associates, in fact, grew stronger from their experiences. They learned how to work with a wide variety of people and deal with them effectively. Now, as they enter a field that

> they may have felt was off-limits to them, those qualities will propel them into leadership roles. They deserve the opportunity to prove their mettle. They deserve a chance.

The B2E Difference

Ours is not the only program seeking to create an alternative pool of tech employees. We have often been asked whether we are just offering another IT boot camp, churning out certificates. Those programs charge a pretty penny—$15,000 is typical—for a short course in some aspect of technology, such as full-stack Java, which, at the moment, is in high demand. Those who go through those programs can check a box that might get them an interview with an HR department, if they are lucky.

When you have to shell out that kind of money to get noticed, it is hard to see how such programs help eliminate barriers to entry. For many people who go through these boot camps, all it does in the long run is cause them to accumulate more debt because they do not ultimately achieve their career goals of landing a position in IT. In fact, we receive many B2E applications from people who have been through boot camps already, and about half of them are accepted into our program.

So what makes us different? We often have been asked that question. Much of the answer lies in the power of our intake system. If you pass that test, we know that you have what it takes to succeed in the IT world, beyond any doubt. You can do it. Now that's not the same as actually going out and doing it. Success requires more than a head for IT. You must have the heart for it, too. You need a powerful work ethic and a strong drive.

Those seem to be built-in qualities among those who apply to our program. Once selected and undergoing the training, very few opt out. Ninety-seven percent of them are hired by York. They are grateful for the opportunity and eager to please. The others have that same attitude but generally have encountered pressing family reasons for being unable to continue.

Our program offers a way in for those who felt left out. A lot of people simply cannot afford a four-year college degree, and no one has ever encouraged them to consider getting one. *College is for other people*, they tell themselves. *I wouldn't fit in there*. Whether real or imagined, those worries hold people back—and our program welcomes them to enter.

If you have the natural ability coupled with the right attitude and work ethic, we can teach you the skills. It doesn't matter if you didn't go to college or if you dropped out without a degree. It doesn't matter if you have never written code. It doesn't even matter if you don't know what IT people do all day. But you can't fake it, any more than you can pretend to be a star athlete if you have two left feet. And yet for every athlete who wins a gold medal, there are many others who might have been winners, too, if they had only had the opportunities. What our program tells them is this: it's never too late.

The Soft Skills Advantage

It takes more than a high IQ to succeed in just about any endeavor under the sun. After launching B2E, we soon saw that the trainees who were quickest to excel were not the same ones who had done the best on our intake testing. Frankly, some of the very best had been on the lower end of the scoring.

Why? I am convinced that success is closely tied to self-awareness. For years I have been a certified trainer in the DiSC personality assessment. This is a tool designed to help people understand how their own natural personality traits impact their ability to work with others and ultimately improve workplace teamwork. I have found that people who excel know their strengths and weaknesses. They understand risks and opportunities. They might have a strong ego, but it is one that takes pride in getting things right and also can admit to being wrong.

It's a lack of that quality that can keep employees from advancing. The way they perceive themselves might be far from how others see them— and that shortsightedness often gets in the way of their success.

That is why our B2E program emphasizes both the hard skills, or technical ability, and the soft skills, or the ability to work effectively with others. We assess applicants for both, and we have ruled some out when the evaluation has indicated that they are not strong team players.

To call people skills soft is a misnomer, because they can be the hardest to master if they don't come naturally. The best golfers in the world are on the driving range every day honing their craft. Likewise, it takes continual practice to develop people skills. Whenever I consult with professionals who have lost their jobs, usually the issue isn't their technical ability. Instead, they need greater self-awareness and a better balance of pride and ego. I have found that the most successful people fully embrace the concept of not having to be the smartest person in the room. Furthermore, communication flow in business, as in life, is very complex. Sharing the right information with the right people at the right time in the right way is of paramount importance. I call this concept the four Rs of success. As simple and repetitive as that sounds, all of us fall prey to this at some point in our lives.

In our program, some trainees who exhibited the strongest interpersonal skills were able to leapfrog over others who rank more highly from a technical standpoint. Their cooperative, helpful nature counted for a large measure of their success. In any job, in any industry, that holds true.

The ones with the people skills, who work well with others, who value teamwork and go out of their way to help others—those are the ones who tend to excel.

It's not a case of black and white. People are complex creatures. At one extreme are brilliant technologists who would rather talk to a machine all day long than talk to a person. At the other end are those who are brilliant with people but not strong technically. The most effective combination lies somewhere in between—and all those skills can be developed. Both the hard skills and the soft skills are teachable for those with the desire to learn.

After completing our program, the newly minted IT associates are assigned to one of our clients. These are remote jobs at companies with offices around the world. The associates do not need to relocate. There's no daily commuting to and from our clients' offices. They can work from their basement or bedroom if they so wish. Some, I am sure, even work in their pajamas sometimes—and they love what they do and make a lot of money doing it.

That's how Relationship Equity works. An act of service, an expression of gratitude, a desire to reciprocate—it often starts that way, small and slow, and then it grows.

In the early days of B2E, I met one-on-one with as many of them as I could, but that became next to impossible as we hired more and more people through the program. However, I continued to meet regularly with a few of them—and why? Because they wrote to me, personally, expressing their gratitude and sharing a bit about their stories and their dreams. They did not ask for those regular meetings. I offered them. I wanted to know more and to see how I might help them. Maybe just by talking, I could help them to sharpen their focus. Perhaps I could connect them with someone in the industry who would accelerate their careers. Most often, the greatest impact was found in the discussions we had pertaining to imposter syndrome. In any case, the act of reaching out, of seeking a deeper connection, put them a step ahead of their peers.

That's how Relationship Equity works. An act of service, an expression of gratitude, a desire to reciprocate—it often starts that way, small and slow, and then it grows. It works on every level.

Selling the Concept

Selling the concept of our B2E program to our clients was as much of a challenge as creating it. Here again, Relationship Equity served us well. It helps to have built a foundation of trust with the person who you hope will sign on to something that is quite out of the ordinary.

The executives who partner with us for IT services tended to be skeptical at first. I knew what they were thinking: *These aren't graduates of a four-year college, and we haven't interviewed them ourselves. How can they be any good?* The bias toward a four-year degree remains strong, and frankly I did get a lot of pushback in the beginning.

If the executives had done the interviewing, though, they likely would have turned down each and every one of our trainees. *Warehouse worker, really? Landscaper? Backhoe operator?* One look at those résumés, and that would be that. I did not hold it against them for having this reaction, as that's the way I initially felt as well. But I had been proven wrong, and I needed to keep the emphasis on what they could do now and moving forward, not on what they had been doing in the past.

To get things going, I approached the highest-ranking IT executives of our biggest clients and basically pitched the program one-on-one. In the end, it was the relationships and trust that I had developed with those executives that encouraged them to try a pilot program. Essentially, I told them this: "I know you've been struggling to find talent, and York has come up with another way for you to get it. Now this might sound a bit crazy, but hear me out. We've worked together a long time, so trust me on this." Then I described B2E and how we had developed it and why. "What we have created here is truly incredible. It's not only life-changing for the people who are brought in, but we're also creating a unique pool of talent that is scalable."

In the Sharing of Our Stories

As we met at a steakhouse to talk about the Barriers to Entry program, the gentleman interrupted me as I began to introduce myself.

"Tell me, where are you from?" he asked as he took a seat.

"Where would you guess?"

"I'd say Northern England," he answered, and I nodded.

I didn't have to ask where he was from. His accent said it all. So I simply broke into song: "True you ride the finest horse I've ever seen!" Delighted, he joined me for a couple of verses of that Christy Moore classic.

It went without saying that I knew where he grew up, and we had ourselves a good laugh. For the next two hours, we shared our stories. He grew up in a very small town in Ireland and worked in a factory for five years before coming to the United States in hopes of discovering the American dream. This was 1988, the same year that I arrived here. He had a heart for finding and encouraging talented people to bring out the best in them. It was obvious within minutes how much we had in common.

It wasn't much of a leap, then, when we began talking about our B2E program. He loved the idea because he understood the concept of the socioeconomic pyramid and that this program was about changing people's lives. It didn't come as much of a shock that his company decided to utilize B2E, but even if they hadn't, I am certain of this: We made a strong connection with a good start on the kind of Relationship Equity that lasts for a lifetime. It's in the sharing of stories that people create the bonds that unite.

Our clients commit from day one to accept a given number of B2E associates who come through our program, so we create customized curriculums in conjunction with our clients and teach skills that are tailored to our client's needs. We don't just teach generic IT skills. We zero in on what our clients require—and they are involved in the curriculum development phase. They speak to the trainees about their company culture, job specifics, and expectations. We work hand in hand to fully prepare the associates who will be working for them. It's a true collaboration, and it goes a long way toward ensuring success on the job.

Our B2E associates go out on contract for one year. Afterward, they can convert to become the client's employee if that is what both the client and the associate desire. That has happened about 90 percent of the time. The aim is to help our clients build their internal staff with highly qualified technical employees. And we don't stop there: our goal is to continue our relationship with those employees, bringing them back for further training on the principles of leadership in the business world.

We launched the program with eight people and were impressed with the quality of their work. A year later, that eight turned into *hundreds* being placed at the majority of our key clients. I continue to be blown away by just how much untapped talent there is, but if you buy into the socioeconomic pyramid, it is easy to see why.

Those clients have reported to us that our associates came to them with enthusiastic attitudes and a can-do approach to their work. Their skills are equivalent to those of college graduates, but they have been around the block a few times. They're not twenty-two years old—for the most part. Many have families. Their life experiences have given them a deep appreciation for how this program can change their trajectory, and that attitude reflects in the quality of their work and how well they work with others.

Despite the early misgivings, the relational bonds that I shared with company leaders were strong enough to dissipate those doubts. They could see my conviction and confidence, and they knew from experience that they could indeed trust me. They agreed to give our program a pilot run—and decided to come back for more. We found ourselves gaining traction quickly, with commitments for dozens of our trainees as soon as they were ready.

As we continue to grow this program, I will increasingly be meeting with executives of major corporations with whom I haven't had the chance to build Relationship Equity yet. It's the success stories that will help to open more of those doors. The program will continue to sell itself as word gets around that we deliver on the promise of quality IT workers who are determined to succeed in a career that they enjoy.

Our clients love our associates because our associates love what they do. They are smart people with wild and wonderful backgrounds, and they often do not realize how much the past informs the present—

and the future that they are building. I have no doubts that in time, as their careers progress and they become senior leaders themselves, many of them will have butt crack stories of their own. It was the *then* that shaped the *now*. As they head out into the wide world of technology, they can draw upon those life experiences to find ways to make all our lives better. They took advantage of an opportunity, and I am eager to see how they will pay it forward.

Shaped by the Past

Jerry was a landscape gardener before coming into the B2E program, and in the winter he shoveled snow, trying to earn enough to feed his family. He was thrilled that our evaluation clearly revealed he could succeed on a tech track, but he had some reservations. "How's a guy like me going to fit in here?" he asked me.

His words struck home. I thought back on my early years and that old familiar feeling that I was an impostor in a place meant for other people, not me.

"Let me tell you something, Jerry," I said, and told him, as I have told so many others, about that cold day long ago in the north of England when I came to my senses while laboring on a scaffold. "The sweat was actually freezing at the base of my spine," I said. Jerry found it very amusing.

"As I think back on those days, Jerry, I realize that they made me who I am. Your life experiences will be a huge advantage to you in ways you can't even imagine yet."

This was a man with a powerful work ethic who was hungry to get ahead in his career. I could see, even if he didn't, what had shaped him that way. Necessity had taught him the value of hard work—and he was about to carry that value forward into a labor of love.

When I go back to our B2E program now, I love spending time with our B2E associates because I can relate firsthand to what they're going through. Their expectations coming into the IT world are low because they never expected they could get into it in the first place. And so anything is a bonus to them right now. It's going to be incredible to watch their journeys over the next few years. A lot of them will end up in leadership positions much faster than they thought they would, because of what they learned in their previous work.

It goes back to me and my bricklaying days. I had no idea what I was really learning at the time. I didn't see that my experiences were teaching me how to deal and work with very different people. Never in a million years did I think that my arse crack story would have a significant impact on an executive's career. The work I did then shaped who I am today.

The same can be said of the individuals in the B2E program. Their lives have been shaping them for success—and though it may be hard for them to see that truth, they will no doubt excel beyond anything they had imagined they could achieve.

7

"WE'RE DOING GOOD TODAY, THANKS."

I have noticed that Americans don't do very well with *good*—grammatically speaking, that is. When I ask people how they're doing today, most of them tell me they're doing good, thanks. To which I feel like saying, "Well, that's great! What did you do for somebody today?"

What they are telling me, of course, is that they are doing *well*, but the mistake is so common that it is probably not even a mistake these days. I just wish that doing good in the world, day by day, was just as common. I believe we each should be looking for opportunities to improve the lives of those around us.

At York Solutions, I preach the philosophy of "doing good while doing well," by which I mean that companies that are doing well should use some of their resources to do good for people so that they, too, have a better chance of doing well. And I also believe in "doing well by doing good," meaning that doing good for others will help us to prosper, too.

Forgive me if that last paragraph was somewhat puzzling, but I won't even try to untangle it because I don't know how I could say it better. What I am expressing is the heart of Relationship Equity: when we reach out to be helpful to others, they likely will want to return the favor in some way, sometime, somehow.

As our Barriers to Entry program has taken root and grown, it certainly has contributed to our company's well-being. It is one way of paying forward the many kindnesses that have been shown to me through the years. I find it gratifying to see how the program has propelled people to success in exciting new careers. Often, they felt like outsiders who did not have a chance of fitting in. They were chained to limited expectations. That was once me.

> When we reach out to be helpful to others, they likely will want to return the favor in some way, sometime, somehow.

I am also proud of our company's commitment to Genesys Works, a national organization with offices around the country that subscribes to the same philosophy upon which we founded the Barriers to Entry program. The nonprofit company's mission is "to provide pathways to career success for high school students in underserved communities through skills training, meaningful work experiences, and impactful relationships."

In the summer before their senior year of high school, students in the program get eight weeks of training. Then they are assigned to work part-time for one of the company's corporate partners as they finish school. In so doing, they can gain the knowledge and skills needed to begin careers in specific technical fields.

The yearlong internships follow an earn-and-learn approach. Not only do the students get paid for their work, which is about twenty hours a week, but also they are contributing highly valued services to the host company. Meanwhile, the program also gives them more than sixty hours of college and career coaching to help them plan for a higher education and a future career path. The counseling includes assistance on how to choose a college and apply to it and how to obtain financial aid. Over 95 percent of those high school students in the program go on to higher education.

A network of Genesys Works alumni provides an additional community of support for the high school students. The alumni, having been through it themselves, can give a wealth of guidance on navigating the academic, social, and financial obstacles that so often threaten to block sustained success.

In its work with inner-city students, Genesys Works comes alongside young people who have been programmed culturally to believe that they are not supposed to have a career but should just go out and get a job. The goal is to break that cycle of thinking and put them on a track to a fulfilling and lucrative future. A lot of these kids are from single-parent households that have been struggling to get by. It is not unusual that the students earn more money during the internship than their parents make. The experience is eye-opening and life-changing.

Kindred Spirits

I have served on the Genesys Works board a lot longer than York has been developing the B2E program. About twelve years ago, I had lunch with the executive director at the time, Jeff Tollefson, a remarkable man who founded Genesys Works' chapter of the Twin Cities of Minnesota. That day, he told me about the organization and how it was changing the trajectories of young people who otherwise might never aspire to anything more than a low-paying, mundane job. At the time, I knew nothing about this nonprofit, but within five minutes I was sold on the concept. This was a mission I understood.

Genesys Works and our Barriers to Entry program are kindred spirits. Genesys Works is geared toward serving a younger crowd, but both reach out into the community to put people on a path to a career to which they might otherwise have had no access. Both emphasize the importance of relationships, skills training, and work experience in IT and business operations. Both focus on networking with others in the field and on professional development.

We have, in fact, accepted some of the young people into our B2E program after they finish their Genesys Works training and internships and graduate from high school. Those who can demonstrate that they have the technical acumen as well as the people skills to succeed are natural candidates for our program. In that way, Genesys Works and York Solutions are partnering in the business of doing good.

York supports the organization in other ways. We contribute every penny from our Link to Leadership program into a scholarship fund for the students. We launched Link to Leadership in 2010 to assist professionals who are at a career crossroads. Often, they are wondering whether to continue their highly technical jobs or to accept an opportunity to advance into positions of management and leadership. Many companies do not offer much training for that transition, so we designed a comprehensive program to provide it—and all of the funds raised as a result go to our scholarship fund to support Genesys Works alumni in their perusal of a college degree to advance its mission.

We are not out to make a profit on our Link to Leadership program. It doesn't affect how well we do in a financial sense. Nor does the annual golf benefit for Genesys Works that we have organized for many years do anything to build our bottom line. We gladly spend our resources to offer those outings, and whatever we bring in, we send back out for the good of our community. We are creating bonds of goodwill. We are building Relationship Equity by reaching out in the spirit of helpfulness—and that, in the end, is what will profit us most of all.

Brimming with Promise

I can close my eyes and see myself as that hardworking young bricklayer in Settle with the shaggy hair and calloused hands. I hear the slosh and scrape of the mortar in the mixer and the laughter and chatter of my mates as we do our work together. It was honest work with good people and for good people. They are with me forever.

I was destined to find another life far afield from my little Northern England town, though nothing of the sort was expected of me, nor did I expect it of myself. I had left school when I was sixteen years old,

> To succeed at anything, you must be willing to work hard, but you need humility to keep that success from going to your head.

knowing only that I would be either a farmer, a factory worker, or a construction worker.

I chose the latter, and I might be laying those bricks to this day—except life happened. I built relationships. I took some chances, met people I might never have otherwise encountered, and moved out into the broader world. My world grew because of the people who crossed my path and encouraged me to try new things.

I know now, though, that I carry a fair portion of that old life with me to this day—and proudly so. In the company of farmers, I learned to be industrious and humble. To succeed at anything, you must be willing to work hard, but you need humility to keep that success from going to your head.

I wonder where I might be now without those early experiences. Would I understand what it is like to feel limited by expectations and circumstances? Would I appreciate how important it is for even just one person to reach out a helping hand to another? Would I want to be that person? Would I be leading a company that embraces that spirit? Would I be able to say to anyone who asked, "Yes, we're doing good today, thanks."

Who you *were* matters because it defines who you *are* and who you *can be*. If you learned by necessity the value of hard work, you are more likely to carry that work ethic forward into a successful career. If you struggled, you are more likely to empathize with those who struggle. And if someone did you a good turn, you are more likely to want to do good for others.

To those newcomers in our Barriers to Entry program who sometimes confide their fear that their past will hold them back, I say this: It can do quite the opposite. Those experiences tend to expand your heart and open your arms to the people around you whose lives you can touch, just as others have touched yours.

And to those young people entering Genesys Works who, on the cusp of adulthood, are just beginning to find their way, I say this: You are breaking through to a bright future brimming with promise. Go boldly and confidently. Your little sisters and brothers are watching you.

FOR BETTER AND FOR WORSE

The water was choppy and sprayed over the skiff as we headed out to North Captiva Island shortly after Hurricane Ian devastated southwest Florida on September 23, 2022. I huddled on a box of emergency supplies, wearing a large set of headphones under my hood, mostly to protect my ears. The spray stung my face and dripped down my nose. My cardboard seat was disintegrating under me. I knew that hours of labor awaited me. Tuning in to some classical music, I slipped into my zone, gazing into the mist. I was drenched. And I was smiling.

With me that blustery afternoon were two boat captains delivering the supplies to the battered island. One of them pointed a thumb at me over his shoulder. "Is he okay?" he asked the other, who laughed in response. "Richard? Yeah, he's loving this. He's like a little boy—he's going to his happy place."

Let me back up now to explain what led to that scene—and how, in late 2019, on the cusp of the coronavirus pandemic, we discovered that wild and wonderful island called North Captiva (not to be confused with Captiva, where a hurricane a hundred years ago tore off a small piece of land that became our little island). When we first came here, we were immediately intrigued by the lack of cars and the off-the-grid feel. It became our home very quickly. And it was there that we would witness the incredible power of Relationship Equity in people's ability to build, and to rebuild, together.

My family fell in love with North Captiva during a ten-day holiday trip there. We found the island so alluring—more like a miniature Costa Rica than anything we had known in the States—that we purchased a home there when the pandemic reared its ugly head. I dubbed it Fantasy Island.

> What matters is the kind of person you are and how you treat others.

Only a third of the island is inhabited, with a few hundred houses; the rest is parkland. Some of the dwellings are modest and others quite lavish, with everything in between. Sandy paths meander through the island, connecting the homes. Accessible only by boat—usually a twenty-minute ferry ride—North Captiva has no cars. Everyone has a golf cart to get around.

Time feels different there. It's island time. Getting on and off the island is not an easy task under normal circumstances, especially considering that *normal* is a word not usually associated with the island. Additionally, all supplies must be delivered by boat. Those of us who spend much time there must adjust to that reality, and we tend to be like-minded in our willingness to accept that way of life. The way I describe it is we are all one sandwich short of a picnic.

We got to know some of those characters as we settled into the island life. They are a mix of seasonal snowbirds, vacationers, and a few year-round residents as well as service providers who compete vigorously for business. Though some of the islanders are quite wealthy, money is not what they talk about. The people do not see one another in terms of wealth or success or title. What matters is the kind of person you are and how you treat others.

Golf Cart Full of Gratitude

Stopping by the tackle shop to pick up some fishing supplies, I overheard a group of four couples who had just arrived for holiday. They were inquiring about renting golf carts so that they could tour the island—but there weren't any available.

I strolled over to them. "Excuse me," I said. "I overheard you talking before. I have two golf carts over at my place that I won't be using today. My wife is off the island for the day."

The gentleman who had been talking to the employee of the rental place turned to me. "Really? I mean, sure—how much?"

"No, I have no need for them today," I explained. "I'm offering for you to take them—if you'd like. "

The group was all smiles. You would have thought I had given them a million dollars. They accepted the offer and drove off, returning the carts late that afternoon looking better than when they had left. They tried to offer me money to show their appreciation, but of course I didn't accept it. The group was deeply grateful, and gratitude has a way of growing.

No doubt those visitors returned home from their holiday with tales about our delightful island and its uncommonly friendly inhabitants. Such is the value of a Relationship Equity mindset. Even the smallest gestures count. When you set out to help people have a better day, they remember, and they mention it to others. The word gets around—and what goes around, comes around.

Our family developed relationships quickly there for the simple reason that we treat everybody the same way—the service providers, the renters, the snowbirds. Whether they have been on the island for twenty years or twenty minutes, it doesn't matter. Nobody is better than anyone else.

Another reason we made connections so readily is my wife Lisa's remarkable way with people. I call her the queen of the island, a title that she does not like. As long as I have known her, I have seen countless people drawn to her because she listens so well and offers solid feedback, challenging them without telling them what to do. She is truly incredible, and why she married me, I'll never know. I do know that it helps that we share that value of treating others as equals. Together we have had so many adventures, for better and for worse.

We saw both the better and the worse at the same time in the autumn of 2022, when Hurricane Ian barreled down on North Captiva. We soon would be witnessing both the wrath of nature and the resilience of humanity. Hoping that our beautiful island would be spared from devastation, we headed down from Minnesota in our truck, stopping for a few nights in Nashville to assess the situation. The news was dismal. The island was being evacuated in anticipation of a storm surge, yet some people were digging in their heels, determined to stay. Lisa spent hours on the phone, imploring everyone we knew there to leave. She found out the time that the last boat was leaving and told them it was now or never. We tuned in to the local news channel serving the island—and the signal cut out. Not a good sign.

At 3:46 a.m., one of the island's full-time residents called us to say that the worst seemed to be over, and we felt a wave of relief. Then we heard from one of our friends who had decided to stay there with her mother. "It was the worst experience of my life," she told us. "The storm ripped part of the roof off my place while we were inside." Her house is only a hundred yards from ours. She sent us a video. The damage to a lot of the houses seemed mostly cosmetic, but many were structurally damaged, and a few, mostly the older ones, were destroyed.

As we drove the rest of the way down, Lisa was still on the phone urging people to get off the island. We stopped on the way to fill our truck and a U-Haul with whatever supplies we could get our hands on—generators, tarps, chain saws, propane, gasoline. These weren't for our own use. We knew there would be great need for those supplies across the island, and not that many people would be able to get down there quickly.

When we arrived, we found that the bridge to one of the marinas that serves the island had washed away. Nonetheless, we managed to find two boat captains who were able to get us home so we could deliver our collection of supplies. As I sat saturated on that cardboard box that day, I felt a weird sense of excitement. Yes, the situation was dire. But I was going to my island. I would be working side by side with my new friends. Even during times of trouble—and, perhaps, especially during such times—relationships can grow deeper.

In the aftermath of the storm, I soon saw that I was not the only one who felt remarkably energized being there. This was not a time for crying. Instead, we felt the camaraderie of a mission to accomplish together. It was time to roll up our sleeves and get boots on the ground. Our mutual predicament called for cooperation and selflessness. We were in this together.

Other homeowners also brought in supplies for the island, and we set up a walkie-talkie communication system because there was no cell signal or electricity of any kind in the beginning. We soon sniffed out a big problem that had to be addressed straightaway. All around the island, the food in freezers and refrigerators was rapidly decomposing—an enticing scent to raccoons and other critters, not so much for humans. We had to get that rotting food into central dumpsters as soon as possible. It was hot and heavy work.

As for our house, the biggest issue was that our sewer pipe had snapped in two. We couldn't use the toilets, nor could we shower—which presented another olfactory challenge. One of the homeowners who had a full-house generator was inviting people over to use their bathroom and kitchen to wash up and prepare meals. Arriving home close to midnight after a visit there, I heard a noise behind our house. A repairman was working on our sewer pipe. He was the father of the boat captain who had wondered whether or not I was okay. Word had gotten around about our need, and this gentleman just showed up and set to work, long after dark, without being asked. It was not an easy job, so I got us a couple of warm beers and helped with the heavy lifting as we laughed together, the time of day almost seeming irrelevant.

That was just one example during those days after the storm where people came to the assistance of others just because they knew there was a need. It demonstrates Relationship Equity in the making. If that gentleman ever were to need my assistance, how willing do you suppose I would be to provide it? *One good turn deserves another* is an old expression because it is a profoundly true one. I would drop everything in a second to offer him whatever help he needed.

One evening we invited one of the boat captains to dinner with us, thanking him for being particularly helpful to us and to so many others during those troubling times. He smiled modestly. "I can't help everybody and be everywhere at the same time," he said, "but I put people like you at the top of my list. You know why? You treat me like I'm one of your family."

That is the spirit that builds communities—people working together, during good times and bad, doing their best to make things better for all. Yes, I was smiling that day on the way to the island as I sat on that skiff, soaked and tired. I understood that people there would be hurting and that there was an overwhelming amount of work ahead of us. But I was there to help and would be with friends, possibly make new ones, and we would be rolling up our sleeves together.

During those days after the storm, the people of North Captiva Island got to know one another at a deeper level and discovered a profound truth: Sometimes a crisis is what brings out the best in people. The bonds that evolved on that island as a result of our mutual challenge will continue to grow, for the betterment of us all.

What the hurricane ordeal demonstrated so clearly was that the principles of Relationship Equity are not confined to the realm of business. They are universally useful in governing every aspect of our lives—our families, our communities, our world. They are as meaningful in a marriage as they are in the marketplace.

> The principles of Relationship Equity are not confined to the realm of business. They are universally useful in governing every aspect of our lives—our families, our communities, our world.

It's often said that we should keep our personal and business lives separate, but in my experience, that can hinder growth, because one influences the other and they often intersect and overlap. I have never adhered to this philosophy, as I have found that the contrary usually results in mutually beneficial outcomes.

In this book, I have talked a lot about the interplay of relationships in the IT industry. Let me assure you, Relationship Equity involves so much more.

Taking It Personally

During a presentation at a global manufacturing firm, we talked about golf for the first twenty minutes. Nothing else. I had come to meet with a top executive about a potential business opportunity, and as I walked into his office, I noticed a picture of the twelfth hole at the Augusta National Golf Club on the wall.

"Have you been to the Masters?" I asked before I had even sat down.

He didn't actually answer my question. Instead, he asked, "Have you played there?" I was shocked to learn that he hadn't been to watch the tournament, but he *had* played there. And so we swapped stories about our shared passion. Business could wait.

After we did get down to business, though, we had plenty other than golf to talk about. His company became a top client. The relationship that we forged that day led to millions of dollars in sales each year for York Solutions.

What is important here is how I got that proverbial seat at the table. It happened as a result of a relationship with another IT executive I had helped after he was laid off during the market slump of 2009. He held the most common position at the time: "in transition." I made an introduction for him that led to his getting a new executive position—this fact, and this fact alone, is what opened the door to ultimately generating millions of dollars in revenue for York for the past fifteen years.

Over the years I have been able to form an extensive network of senior executives who are quite willing to meet with people on my recommendation. They trust that I have their best interests at heart and would not be wasting their time. Again, that level of credibility did not just happen accidentally. A lot was going on in the background—namely, the building of Relationship Equity, and much of that came from an awareness of others' needs and a willingness to help without any expectation of getting something in return. While some may consider my time spent as free consulting, I would consider it as Relationship Equity development. Imagine it like a healthy, growing tree—the bigger and stronger the tree, the deeper the roots. As long as the tree continues to be fed, it will keep growing, and its roots will become stronger and deeper.

Life isn't all about business, but business is all about life. It ruffles my feathers to hear people say, "It's just business; don't take it personally"— because the personal touch is what matters most.

Just Ask Questions

I once asked my father-in-law, a wonderful man whose shoes are always well polished, what was going through his mind that day long ago when his daughter introduced me, a long-haired freak from England wearing rugby shorts. "My first thought," he answered, "was *Lisa, what the hell are you thinking?*" He smiled. "And then I got to know you."

Lisa has the best qualities of both her parents. She treats people fairly and warmly because she was brought up that way. Her dad spent years as an executive in human resources, hardworking and strong-willed. After devoting her early adulthood to her children, Lisa's mum went back to school in her fifties to finish her four-year degree and acquire a master's degree at the same time. She then worked for many years in a shelter for abused women, selflessly devoting hours to helping others. Both her parents emphasized the value of family—and that is a trait that we share in our marriage.

I owe it to Roy Brammer, my brother from another mother, that Lisa and I ever met. I have known Roy since I came to America to teach golf at the camp near Philadelphia back in 1989. He is from South Africa and was there to teach tennis. Today, Roy is the chief operating officer at York—so clearly we built plenty of Relationship Equity in the years between. Let me fill in some of the blanks.

We had quite an eclectic team from around the world at the Haverford College camp. One day a Scottish lad named McTavish came up to me and said, "I need your help. This heathen hit me in the face last night, for no reason, just out of the blue. He's from South Africa, and I said something he didn't like, and without warning, he punched me in the face. I want you to go and sort him out."

Next morning at breakfast, McTavish pointed out the fella who had hit him. We approached him, and I introduced myself with

McTavish peering over my shoulder. "I understand you had a bit of an altercation last night," I said. "What happened?"

"That idiot peering over your shoulder was way out of line," Roy answered. "He was spouting crap about apartheid, and he had no idea what he was talking about, just kept spouting off rubbish. I warned him a couple times to shut up or I'd knock him out. He opened his mouth again, and … I put him in his place."

I turned to McTavish. "You got what you deserved, mate." I sat down to join Roy Brammer for breakfast—and, as Roy always adds when I tell that story, "we've been best friends ever since."

The moral of the story? Ask questions before you act and get the truth on the table. After the camp, Roy returned to school at Oral Roberts University in Tulsa, Oklahoma. I had a couple of days to kill before going back to England, so I did some traveling—including a trip to Tulsa to see Roy again before I left. We were out at a bar one evening when I noticed a beautiful young lady, and, of course, I made my way over.

"My name is Lisa," she said, and, upon hearing my accent, she added, "Are you from Australia?"

"Australia!" I shouted and put my hands around her throat, pretending I was going to strangle her. I'd probably had one pint of Guinness too many at that point.

"Oh!" she said. "I guess not."

And that was the start of it. I soon was telling friends that I had met the girl I was going to marry. The following summer, Lisa and I arranged to work together at a summer camp in Florida. After ten wonderful weeks at that camp, we drove in her car to visit her parents in Saint Louis. When we pulled into the driveway, she pressed a little button, and the garage door opened. I had never seen such a thing. It blew my mind. And the garage was attached to the house.

It was like something from a movie.

Much water having gone under the bridge, I finally bought a ring and flew back to the States, planning to ask Lisa to marry me on Easter weekend, 1991. I had been feeling sick, but she wondered if I was faking it to get out of going to church. When I felt a bit better, I took her to a fancy restaurant to pop the big question—but chickened out. On the way home, we stopped at a grocery store for some medicine—and standing at the checkout line, in front of a big display of condoms, I put my hand in my pocket and without thinking pulled out the ring—so I guess that came across as my proposal. I'll never forget her exact words: "Get me out of here. I'm going to throw up!" I took that as a no, but she was really just in shock.

In hopes of spending some more concentrated time together, Lisa flew back to England with me to see if we would be compatible for life. Bearing in mind that Lisa is a cautious and critical decision maker about everything, this method of proposing may not have been my brightest idea.

Months later, as I was watching TV one night, she came up behind me and poured a full plate of spaghetti Bolognese over my head and packed her bags to head out the door. I took that as a definite no. If I am being honest, I cannot recall what I said that prompted that response, but I am sure it was well deserved.

Pasta and all, two years later, she said yes, and we married, on January 2, 1993, in Saint Louis, Missouri. Our early days together were lean. I recall searching under the couch cushions for coins to pay the bus fare and ended up finding so many that we were able to share a pack of crisps and a bar of chocolate that day. But with time and dedication, worse turned to better, and we worked together through life's trials and tribulations as they came along. Namely, our very much unplanned pregnancy with our firstborn happening when neither of us was employed.

Today, after three decades of marriage, I have learned two indisputable facts: My wife is always right, and I am always wrong. Those are the two rules, so far as I can see, for how to build a strong and enduring marriage. When I told Lisa that one of the chapters in this book on Relationship Equity would include some thoughts on how it works in marriage, she smirked: "Oh yeah? Let *me* write *that* chapter!"

All kidding aside, though, the principles of Relationship Equity clearly are of supreme importance in a healthy marriage and family life. As in business, I have learned not to jump right in with my solution to every problem. Often when people call me at the office with a problem, I ask outright whether they want my advice or just want me to listen, and it is often the latter. I have found that the best way to help people get to the truth is to just ask questions. That's how it is in a marriage relationship, too. Lisa deserves the dignity of coming to her own conclusions and making her own decisions. Besides, she doesn't often need my advice because she's much smarter than me.

What matters immensely is that we stand together in our values. We both believe that family comes first, and everything else is a distant second. And as I wake up each day, the first thing I think is this: *What can I do to make this day better for my wife?* Even if it's just making the bed or emptying the dishwasher, how can I go out of my way to be a help to her? And when I do those things, I find that she is all the more eager to find ways to make my day better, too. That's the spirit that makes any kind of relationship grow.

Thirty years later, I still ask her on a regular basis why she ever agreed to marry me. When I met her, this brilliant and lovely woman's boyfriend was the captain of the American football team at the University of Tulsa. And she dropped him for a rough-hewn Yorkshire bricklayer? Maybe it's that old impostor syndrome rearing up in me again, but I still shake my head in wonder. To this day, I ask her the same question her father did when he met me: "What were you *thinking*?"

CONCLUSION: A WEALTH OF POSSIBILITY

Young people turn their attention mostly toward what *will* be. That's still the case for me, but I increasingly find myself, as the years pass, reflecting on what *was*. That's particularly so when I am out on the golf course with my buddy Tom Fleming, who has nearly a century to reflect upon.

Tom is ninety-six as I write this, and he knows it. He is at the point where he can see his legacy defined—and it's a grand one, for sure. Spending time with Tom has led me to ponder how mine will be defined. This thing called life is an adventure and should be treated as one.

For well over a decade, I have spent more time on the links with Tom than with anyone else on earth. Why so? There's no business reason. He did own and run a successful company, and I have learned a lot from him about running my own—but that isn't why I want to play golf with him.

It was 2010 when I met Tom. I recently had joined the Minneapolis Golf Club while getting over a concussion. (I fell off a chair at a coffee shop, never mind how.) I had been laid up for months and badly needed to get out and about, doing something fun. *And that would be golf,* I thought. *I am a golfer!* Out on the first tee one day, I approached an elderly gent to ask if I could join him. He peered at me and extended his hand. "What's your name?"

"Richard Walker."

"Never heard of you," he said flatly. "Who'd *you* ever fight?" And I knew then and there that this was my kind of fella.

Tom grew up in a rough section of Philadelphia but refused to be limited by circumstances. He served his country, went to Penn State on the GI Bill, worked for years at an engineering company, then built his own company with those skills.

And he had something else going for him, too. He liked people, and people liked him. I soon realized that Tom knows everybody at the club, and they all know and love him. He has been a club member since 1959, but the reason for their affection has nothing to do with golf. They could tell he is as authentic as they come, a genuine friend. He is a master at the art of Relationship Equity.

Tom is a great storyteller, funny and gregarious, but he never talks about himself and his accomplishments unless I ask him questions. Usually, though, it's Tom who is asking the questions. He is genuinely curious about people. He asks about my family, my business, my ideas, my perspectives.

In short, Tom has approached life with a sense of adventure. He pulled himself up from a challenging start in life and stepped boldly through the doors that opened for him, saying yes to opportunities. Along the way, he gained a lot of technical and business ability, but his greatest skill is his way with people. He shows he cares and is ready to help, without any expectations. Tom is the embodiment of much of what I have been trying to get across in this book.

That's why I have played so much golf with Tom Fleming. The two of us, in our way of looking at the world, are pretty much one and the same. Just a few years ago, I had the great pleasure, and yes, honor, of going to the Masters with Tom. Many of my friends complimented me on doing such a gracious thing, as if I was doing it for Tom. What they didn't realize was that I was actually doing it for *me*, knowing that this was likely the only time Tom would get to experience the tournament in person. Along with us was our dear friend Loyal Bud Chapman, whom I also played many rounds of golf with over the years. Bud was a legend in golf for many reasons and has since passed away at the age of ninety-seven. The experience I had with them both that weekend will stay with me forever. They were each like little boys on Christmas Eve the moment we entered the hallowed grounds of Augusta National. I will cherish those moments forever.

In the Business of Humanity

As I continue to reflect on years past, I think again of another incredible person with whom I share a worldview. When Bill Carr and I first started our partnership, he made it clear that the people we served—our employees—were the soul of our business. Bill and I have quite different skill sets—we complement each other effectively—but we are alike on what matters most. To this day, humanity is the core of our business.

The relationships we forge with others are of supreme impor-

> The relationships we forge with others are of supreme importance. When you get those right, the rest follows.

tance. When you get those right, the rest follows. If you are a friend who is genuine, you will have genuine friends—and, lo and behold, they will want to help you just as you have helped them. We need one another. We are not islands unto ourselves.

That's not something you can fake. People know if you authentically like them. My colleague Emily joined our company seeking opportunities for growth, having felt frustrated by the limitations at her previous employer. Off to a great start, she proudly showed me a chart of how much Relationship Equity she had developed with a client. "That's great!" I said. "Now tell me, how much do you have with your peers at York?"

The question lit a fire under her. She knew the value of building relationships and realized that she needed to do so in her new workplace, too. She went out of her way to be helpful to her colleagues, and that dynamic energized her career. Emily found the opportunity for the growth that was her heart's desire.

Only when that outreach is genuine, as it is with Tom and Bill and Emily, will the equity in relationships grow. If it isn't authentic, it comes across as obsequious, which is a big word that describes someone or another we all have known and sometimes label with less polite terms. Genuine friends are not looking for a payback. It is simply their nature to give of themselves, desiring to pay forward the good things that have come their way.

The Common Denominators

In this book, we have examined the elements of Relationship Equity. These are the qualities that lead to productive careers and fulfilling lives. In my time, I have observed common denominators among people who turn the corner to success:

- They approach life not fretfully but expectantly, eager for possibilities and willing to take some risks.
- When those possibilities present themselves, they look for how they can say yes to them, not for excuses to say no.
- They are willing to work hard to make the most of what comes their way. In fact, they enjoy working hard.
- They exhibit a cooperative, helpful spirit that focuses on the interests of the group, not on the self-interests of the individual.
- Thinking in terms of *us*, not *me*, they are eager to build enduring relationships, expecting nothing in return.
- They know the right things to say at the right time, to the right people, in the right way. They ask pertinent questions and avoid intrusive ones.
- They find common ground on which to launch a relationship, and they take the time to nurture it properly.
- They break free of limitations imposed by others, often by society itself.
- They break free, as well, of limitations that they may have imposed on themselves—those inner voices saying, *That's not for me, I don't fit in here, I'm not good enough.*
- They have gained the confidence to fit in wherever they wish, no longer feeling like impostors but rather as heirs to good fortune.
- They value their past and their life experiences, realizing that they have gained strength from challenges.
- They have learned that it is hard to control what others say and do but that they always have the freedom to choose how to respond.
- They choose kindness and helpfulness as their modus operandi.

The winners in this world are those who make it their business to reach out to others and treat them with dignity. Good things come to those who do good. That has been the prevailing theme in this book, chapter after chapter. I hope that these words will endure after I am long gone to encourage people to think and act differently as they make their way in this world. If this book serves to change even one life for the better, I will count it a success.

Good fortune has come my way over and over during my years on this spinning globe, and most of it has been by way of the people I have been privileged to know. I could not have asked for a better mother and father, or brother and sister, who epitomize the true value of family and proved to me that everything else in life is a distant second. To my family and friends and all those who helped me along, I am eternally grateful.

> The winners in this world are those who make it their business to reach out to others and treat them with dignity. Good things come to those who do good.

In those early years in the hills and dales of home, I learned the foundations of good living, though I had no idea how well those lessons would serve me. My father's voice echoes through the years: *Nobody is better than you, Richard, and you're no better than them. Some just have better skills.* Those words are as fresh to me now as they were when I was a boy. So is the sense of adventure that my mother carries with her and the grit with which she tackles life.

As relationship after relationship brought me to where I am today, I now have the privilege of paying forward that good fortune. At the end of the day, when I'm hanging up my boots, I want to look back and know that I built a strong foundation for my family as well as a solid company devoted to helping people attain those better skills—for the benefit of themselves, their families, their communities.

In every new encounter is a wealth of possibility, just waiting to be tapped.

ADDENDUM: "NOTHING SHORT OF A MIRACLE"

In chapter 6, I described our Barriers to Entry program at York Solutions as life-changing and gave a few examples of how it had launched exciting new careers in IT. Here are a few more stories of program participants who pursued opportunities that they might otherwise never have found. See for yourself how B2E is putting people on a trajectory for success.

Dee Hampton

My childhood was a tough childhood. It was full of a lot of hardship, it was full of a lot of pain, but one thing it was full of also was a lot of love.

Growing up, Dee Hampton lived in an environment filled with hardships—family struggles, violence, drug abuse, and more. Though her mother loved and supported her, Dee faced many obstacles, including constantly moving and enrolling in new schools.

When Dee was thirteen, she relocated to Inglewood, California, to spend time with her father but quickly learned that the community was a hotbed of drug and gang activity. She later moved back to live with her mother in Colorado, but the family still struggled with expenses and turmoil.

Through that time, Dee maintained exceptional grades and pursued extracurricular activities. School was an escape, and she was able to begin a high school curriculum right out of sixth grade, skipping two years.

As the pressures at home worsened, Dee contacted her uncles so that she and her two siblings could have a safe place to live without being split up. Then, when she was in eleventh grade, she discovered she was pregnant. At age eighteen, she was now responsible for another life, on top of the parenting role she had taken on with her siblings. As priorities shifted, Dee did what she always had done—prevailed.

As her family grew through the years to six children, Dee dedicated her life to ensuring they would have every opportunity to succeed. She worked tirelessly to provide for them. In addition, Dee also sought to help those in her community. Whether through her nonprofit work or the outreach programs at a church, Dee did whatever she could to improve others' lives.

Many years later, when she had only one child left at home, Dee learned of the Barriers to Entry program. Friends told her that it seemed right for her and that she was made for something different, where her helping hand would reach more people. She was hesitant, as most people are, but eventually applied, interviewed, and was accepted into the program.

While Dee was driving to her second day of training, her car engine exploded. But nothing would stand in her way. She mapped out a bus route and set off. Five buses later, she arrived. Getting to the training class each day became a grueling commute of nearly three hours, but Dee knew how to adapt to what had to be done. She kept up that schedule for the entire three weeks of training. That heart, that pure determination and grit, is not something that can be taught in a classroom.

After the training program ended, Dee was placed at a great company. She went to work eager to learn but still feeling like an imposter. On her first day, she ran into multiple people she knew from past work experiences—and Dee started to realize this was where she was meant to be. She could do this.

Dee asked questions and networked constantly, looking for any opportunity to grow. Before long, she was shadowing scrum masters, sitting in on meetings, and taking notes so that she could go home and teach herself anything that was unfamiliar. Dee went beyond what anyone expected of her. After a year and a half in that role, she took over the training program she previously shadowed and continued to excel. She returned to York Solutions to become a community outreach manager—touching the lives of others, as she had been doing for a lifetime.

Dee refuses to take a back seat while others do the driving, and that is what the B2E program is all about. The candidates are used to working hard and proving themselves time and time again—and they *want* to work hard. It excites them. It gives them hope for a chance at something they had thought unattainable. They are the kind of people who, if their car went up in flames, would stare at it not in defeat but wondering, *Okay, so now what's the best way to get to work?*

Adjetevi Adjety-Bahun

This whole thing [B2E] is nothing short of a miracle ... I've told everybody I know that if you want to get into IT, this is your path.

Adjetevi Adjety-Bahun grew up in Togo, a country in West Africa. In 2013, when he was twenty-three years old, Adjetevi received a lottery visa to be able to move to the United States, which he saw as an opportunity for a better education and improved living conditions.

After landing in Minnesota in the dead of winter, Adje quickly realized that his English was better on paper than in person. He didn't have a phone and needed to contact his uncle—but how could he even ask those around him for help? With a little creativity, he got in touch with him and began his new life in the States.

Adje wasted no time. His uncle had a connection at Burlington Coat Factory. It took a month for Adje's government documents to arrive, but as soon as he was eligible, he began work there. He also took a night job at Saint Jude's Hospital, doing medical assembly. He was living on four hours of sleep, but he was determined to save enough to attend Hennepin Technical College, near Minneapolis, without a student loan. He knew he wanted a career involving computers.

With hard work, Adje finished his coursework, but he struggled to find a job—and when he finally found one, it wasn't what he had hoped for. Then he learned of the Barriers to Entry program. He felt torn: *Should I do this? Should I risk leaving the job that took me so long to find?* The opportunity seemed too good to be true—but Adje decided to take the chance.

James Allen

*It wasn't really for certain that I was going to be able
to go to college, just because I was always helping out
with the family. We were always financially struggling.
It wasn't on the radar ... so I just started working.*

The oldest in a family of eight children, James Allen had to grow up much faster than most. He had a loving and hardworking mother but no reliable father figure, so James stepped into that role for his siblings. He started work at age twelve. Even as a preteen, he knew the reality of his situation and decided to do something about it.

James excelled in his classes and had a passion for music. He realized that it wasn't in the cards for him to go to college. The high cost, as well as his family responsibilities, made it unattainable for him. So he got a retail job right out of high school and continued to support his family financially and emotionally. He did well in retail and felt a sense of financial security.

After a few years, James decided to go back to school. Not only did he want a better-paying career but also he wanted his siblings to see the value of education. He wanted to pave a path for them to follow. So he took out loans to pursue his passion for music. After trying one college that wasn't the right fit, he decided to move across the country and go to a specialized school in Minnesota. That decision would be the catalyst for many life changes.

While at that school, James continued working in retail but realized he had hit his glass ceiling. He began looking for corporate jobs but found that most employers required four-year degrees. So he kept his focus on his education, completing his bachelor's degree in music and business.

Even with his four-year degree, James couldn't find what he was looking for. Then a friend examined his résumé and recognized that it didn't adequately highlight his skill set. Another friend who had been through the B2E program suggested he would be a perfect candidate for it. James was skeptical. *IT isn't my wheelhouse*, he thought, *but what have I got to lose?*

Upon entering the program, James quickly showed he had the skill set to succeed. He felt discouraged at first. His peers seemed to know more about the subject matter than he did. Instead of withdrawing, he worked all the harder. Once he was placed in an IT job, he began to feel confident. He learned quickly, and the higher-ups in the company noticed. James felt inspired to share what he was learning with his fellow B2E associates and coworkers. He created materials to help others acclimate to their new roles. This was a big turning point for him.

Along the way, James cultivated relationships that helped to advance his career. He became an indispensable member of many IT teams and the head of one of them. He took a career path quite different than he had ever imagined. He was earning twice what he ever made in retail.

James came to believe in himself and his abilities. It wasn't that he lacked the grit to succeed in whatever he did. He had plenty of that, but life had put obstacles in his way that demanded his attention and that at times seemed insurmountable—and James had overcome.

Jon Pederson

I am connected with a community that is encouraging and has also done it. It is a lot easier to believe that you can do it when you are surrounded by people who are doing it.

When Jon Pederson was in high school, he had a great love for computers. He excelled in his classes, but when he moved on to college, he found that everything was different. He wasn't performing well and didn't feel that he was getting much out of it, so he decided to start working instead.

After about a year of doing various jobs, Jon was recruited by the Marine Corps. He signed on for six years, intending to finish his education after he got out. Back in civilian life, a friend recommended the B2E program, and he decided to give it a go.

During his years as a marine, Jon's confidence grew and his problem-solving abilities improved. When he entered the IT field, those two traits became his greatest assets and the game changer for his career. He had needed a means to translate those traits into something tangible for his résumé—and that's what the B2E program did for him. Jon built his skill set and advanced quickly. His financial position improved dramatically, allowing him to pay off the mortgage to his family's home, which he had never expected to do so early in life.

Dasha Ryzhenkova

When I got the phone call, I was so excited. Finally, something is happening, something exciting that will get me somewhere. It's not just a job; it's a career. It's a new life.

Born and raised in Ukraine, Dasha Ryzhenkova moved to Iowa when she was fifteen, knowing only basic English that she improved using the Rosetta Stone software. At first she had trouble adapting. The people here were not the most welcoming, she felt, and she was facing some family hardships. Nonetheless, she did well in school. With few friends, she focused on her studies and found opportunities she didn't have at her small school in Ukraine.

Dasha wanted to study engineering in college and started off ambitiously, taking eighteen credits in her first semester while pursuing her goal of learning seven languages. It was too much for her, she realized, so she took a step back from school after her first year.

Deciding that she needed a change of scenery, Dasha moved to Minnesota to be close to a friend and started working at Jamba Juice, developing the skills to advance quickly. After a few other retail positions, she got a job at the Department of Motor Vehicles, then for a while at a car dealership.

Dasha wanted more than just a job. She wanted a meaningful career—and she found it in the B2E program. A friend who was in the program suggested it to her, and she jumped at the opportunity. She passed the test, began training, and excelled. She was placed in a position at Optum and launched a career with far more potential than she had ever hoped to find.

Helen Lindberg

I'm in a position now where I am going to be able to buy a house in a year. I never thought that I would be able to do that on my own.

Helen Lindberg attended four high schools in three years, and despite her fragmented schooling, she held on to a passion for computers, video games, and coding. After it turned out that traditional schooling was not a good fit for her, Helen decided to get her GED.

For seventeen years after that, Helen worked in the food industry, starting at a Rochester coffee shop. She found that her skills were a match for that line of work. She was coffee shop manager for eleven of those years. In that position, she developed and strengthened a variety of skills—problem solving, time management, delegation of tasks, customer service—that would be crucial in a career that she was not yet pursuing.

After the birth of her child, Helen wanted to make a career change. As a single mum, she yearned for more dependable hours and sufficient pay to raise her daughter. She wanted to set a good example for the girl.

After doing some research, Helen devoted a lot of time and money to complete a coding boot camp through the University of Minnesota. Despite many interviews, though, she still struggled to find an IT job that was the right fit. She wanted a position that would offer training so that she wouldn't be overwhelmed by a new set of responsibilities.

That was where the B2E program came in. Helen aced the entrance test and began her B2E training. Soon she was working at Best Buy, enjoying her free time with her daughter, and finally feeling financially stable.

Kelsey Johnson

You can be anything you want to be.

After graduating from Mississippi State University, Kelsey Johnson was a sixth-grade teacher for a few years before a tornado hit their town and killed her aunt. She moved to New Orleans and taught on a naval base while also teaching community college courses on the side.

She eventually moved back to Mississippi to be with her mother, who was having health complications. Kelsey needed a job but felt she should try something different and wanted it to be a work-from-home position.

"You can be anything you want to be," Kelsey often told her kids. She realized she should be taking her own advice—and she got what she wanted in the B2E program, which led her to a position at Optum.

Kelsey found a new line of work that she loved.

Shuelong Moua

*I paid for training just like this and still didn't find a
job. Now they want to pay me for training?*

When Shuelong Moua was in high school, he lacked confidence in his intelligence. The thought of studying IT in college intrigued him, but he didn't think he was smart enough. Instead, he served six years in the National Guard as a combat engineer. Shue then pivoted to the restaurant industry because he wanted to make a change and loved to cook. During his years in that field, he was a cook, a server, and a manager.

After suffering an injury, Shue was unable to walk for a year, so he started a desk job in customer service. This was a turning point for him because it helped him to realize that he had more intellectual skills than he gave himself credit for. He decided to attend a coding boot camp through the University of Minnesota. He wasn't able to secure a job in the field, however, so he went back to customer service work.

About a year later, Shue's cousin told him about the B2E program. At first he was a little apprehensive but decided he didn't have anything to lose. He gave it a shot—and ended up with a full-time position at Best Buy.

ACKNOWLEDGMENTS

To my father, Richard Walker II: I can only hope my three kids have half as much respect for me as I do for you. In my book (metaphorically speaking), you are without a shadow of a doubt the wisest man on the planet. You see and hear things that nobody else does. You taught me at a very young age the power of lateral thinking, always challenging conventional wisdom and never taking things at face value. That way of thinking has played a big role in our company's success. But above all, you taught me that no matter what, family always comes first. And everything else is a distant second.

To my mother, Luigina: There isn't any mother on earth who has devoted her life to her family as much as you have. The only thing that has ever mattered to you is family. I'll never know how you didn't turn and run back to your family in southern Italy when you got to the border in Germany. I can only imagine what was going through your mind when you heard people speaking a completely different language that you didn't even know existed. And how you managed to find your way to Settle, England, at such a young age is truly incredible. Your grit, resilience, and perseverance are almost incomprehensible.

To my sister, Gillian: First and foremost, thank you for looking out for me in my early adulthood. Even though you were (and still are) three years younger than me, you were always the most sensible of the three of us! I'm not sure I've ever paid you back for all those times you subsidized me at the pub when I ran out of money! I can't tell you just how proud I am of you with all that you have accomplished. You took the bull by the horns at a very young age and don't seem to be slowing down anytime soon. Thank you for who you are. You have always been the rock in the family.

To my wife, Lisa: Where do I start? As I've already said in this book, I will never know why you said yes that day on January 2, 1993. But I'm very glad you did. We have had one hell of a ride since we met in Tulsa, Oklahoma, all those years ago. You have influenced my life in so many ways, some obvious and some maybe not so obvious. You have always believed in me, even when I didn't believe in myself. You have stood by me through thick and thin, and we've had plenty of both. I have no idea where the rest of our life's adventures are going to take us, but as long as I'm with you, I know we have one hell of a fun ride ahead of us. And whatever I said that caused you to pour a plate of spaghetti Bolognese over my head many years ago, I'm sorry!

To my Gingey (Hannah): I'll never forget what happened on March 19, 1995. You entered this crazy world. Our firstborn. It was as if the world stood still for a brief moment in time to recognize the arrival of the most important new human on the planet. You were an absolute miracle and still are. I have absolutely no doubts that you are going to have a significant impact on humanity with your intelligence and passion. Think yourself lucky that you got most of your mother's genes. Although I'm very sorry to have passed on my ginger genes! But you can't have everything.

To my Billy: You were the happiest baby on the planet. And that hasn't changed one bit as you've become a fine young man. When you were seven years old, one of your teachers told us at a school conference how you always went out of your way to help other kids in your class, without being asked to. And I'm very happy that your desire and willingness to help others has stuck with you throughout your life. It's rare that a father can call his son his best friend, but that you are. I will never take that for granted and know that won't change for the rest of my life.

To my Allison: I'm not sure how or why it happened, but you have been my number one advisor in just about every aspect of my life since you were fourteen years old. Wise beyond your years is the understatement of all understatements. I'm so proud of the young woman you have become, refusing to conform to societal pressures. You are paving your own way, and I have absolutely no doubt, like your older brother and sister, you will make a significant impact in this world. I can't wait to read your book and can't thank you enough for being my advisor and key editor for my book. You and only you could have pulled that off, as, unfortunately for you, you think more like me than anybody else on the planet. In fact, you often know what I'm thinking before I do!

There are countless other people I could call out who have positively impacted my life. In fact, there are just too many to mention in this book. So I'm going to stick with the people who have had the most influence, and that's my family. I love you all!

To my editors, I extend my gratitude for your dedication, expertise, and invaluable contributions to this book. In particular, to my Allison: your meticulous editing, insightful feedback, and unwavering commitment have shaped the book into its final form. The teamwork, communication, and belief in this project have been truly inspiring.